Winning Partnership

India–UK Relations
Beyond Brexit

Edited By

Manoj Ladwa

© Individual Contributors

First published 2017
ISBN 978-1-9997651-0-1

Published by

India Inc. Limited
E:info@indiaincorporated.com   W: indiaincorporated.com

Contents

BUSINESS VOICES

INTRODUCTION

The Makings of a Winning Partnership

Manoj Ladwa

A Return to the Roots

A little more than four centuries ago, in 1612 AD, Sir Thomas Roe, ambassador of Queen Elizabeth I, had presented his credentials to Emperor Jehangir and sought his blessings to establish trade relations with what was then the richest empire in the world. He represented a country that was itching with ambition and itching for an alternative to what it considered stifling engagement with the prevailing powers of Europe. (That may sound familiar but let us not get ahead of the story!)

Thomas Roe's voyage to India marked the formal beginning of a bilateral relationship that would go through numerous twists and turns, see many ups and downs, endure severe strains and emerge, in the latter half of the twentieth century, as a template for a mature relationship in a postcolonial world. The British influence on India is all too evident—the English language, the passion for cricket, the Westminster system of government and a legal system largely modelled on the one in the UK. Less discussed, but equally visible is the reverse culinary colonisation—of a British people who have voluntarily accepted the ubiquitous 'curry' as their de facto national dish.

To commemorate four centuries of civilisational cross-pollination, the two countries have decided to celebrate 2017 as the Year of Culture. This is a fitting tribute to mutually accommodative and individually vibrant cultural histories on the occasion of the seventieth anniversary of Indian independence.

But culture, soft power and warm people-to-people ties are only one part of the multifaceted relationship between the two nations. Following the UK's decision to leave the European Union and British Prime Minister Theresa May's letter to the EU Council triggering Article 50 of the Lisbon Treaty, the British government needs to demonstrate, in no uncertain terms, that it can find alternative markets and potentially tie up trade deals that compensate for the losses that could accrue from Brexit. And that is why this may be a good time for the UK and India to announce that they are BFF (best friends forever, in social media language).

The UK as a global financial powerhouse and technological leader can find many synergies with India, the world's fastest-growing major economy, with a billion-plus aspirational consumers. I have witnessed first-hand the synergy and energy that the trade and investment relationship brings, having for many years practised as a dual-qualified English solicitor and Indian advocate—supporting over 500 UK companies invest or do business in India, and many India companies set up and enter the UK market. This unique vantage point on trade, investment and the intersection with policy, politics and diplomacy, only makes me more positive about the future.

But it will be a big mistake to look at this unique relationship in purely transactional terms. The truth is that the shared values that many observers, analysts and well-wishers talk about go well beyond the tired clichés that surface when politicians run out of issues to talk about.

The UK–India relationship has all the ingredients of a winning partnership, but much more needs to be done and fast. Let me set out a few milestones:

- The relationship is decisively entering the 'post postcolonial' era.
- The pendulum of influence in the relationship has swung; it is now much more a relationship of equals than at any time in the last two-and-a-half centuries, leading to questions about who actually needs who more.
- Alongside global Britain, we are also seeing the emergence of a global India, and both countries recognise that their futures lie in more,

not less, engagement with the global community and also with each other.

But potential is one thing; its realisation quite another. To do justice to the immense potential of this relationship, both London and New Delhi need to take a series of concrete actions such as:

- Leveraging the potential of their combined soft power on the world
- Allowing freer market access of people and services
- Deeper engagement with the Indian view on immigration/trade
- Understanding the UK government's stand on immigration
- Reimagining the Commonwealth and coordination through other multilateral institutions
- Embracing fully the capabilities of the City of London in financing India's growth ambitions

These can form an enabling architecture for the India–UK relationship to reach its full potential.

UNDERSTANDING EACH OTHER

Over the past two decades, UK–India ties have transformed from a patron–client relationship to one where India has slowly but steadily clawed back to equal status. But...there's always a 'but' when one makes such sweeping statements...India still, admittedly, looks at Britain as a source of high technology and defence platforms and Indians still hold British institutions of higher education in esteem—sending thousands of students every year for graduate, postgraduate and technical studies—but the growing perception (at least) of Britain pulling up the drawbridge on Indian talent has not gone down well as is evident from the falling numbers of Indian students choosing British universities for higher studies in recent years. This will have a long-term and negative effect on relations.

The oft-cited 'special relationship' will remain a buzzword without substance if the two governments do not display a 'special understanding' of each other's compulsions and goals. But this deep and emotional relationship between the countries has been allowed, by successive governments, to drift and settle into a shallow transactional one, with the focus firmly on 'quantity' rather than the quality of the relationship.

Brexit has brought about a decisive break in this convenient, albeit highly limiting, world view. Things have now changed. India has changed, the UK has changed and the power dynamic that defined the relationship between these two countries has changed. So, it naturally follows that the rules of engagement should also change in line with ground realities.

What are the new rules of engagement? There are at least five:

- Move from the special and/or strategic relationship to call it a truly global partnership. A global Britain must embrace a global India and its aspirations on the world stage.
- Have a clear mission statement that will inspire and drive the relationship; this needs to define what winning looks and feels like for both countries.
- Leverage the power of the Indian diaspora in the UK and the shared values keeping in mind Prime Minister Modi's outreach to them and his description of people-to-people connects as the 'Living Bridge' between countries.
- Invest in shared prosperity, rather than haggle over short-term 'what's-in-it-for-me' benefits; engage in a more genuine open dialogue that shakes off the stifling baggage of formality; and stop shadow-boxing over ephemeral issues.
- Learn from the lessons of the past while respecting our shared history; but emphasise much more on our shared future—two great nations, one glorious future.

The Elephant in the Room

The rise of China looms large as the elephant in the room, especially when it comes to India's neighbourhood and its economic, political and strategic relationships with other big powers. The UK has its own understandable reasons in pursuing greater cooperation on a range of issues with China but there is some wariness in India about how London will react if it has to choose between Beijing and New Delhi on any issue of strategic importance or dispute. Ideally, the UK would not want to choose.

India, under Prime Minister Modi, has made it clear that it is uncomfortable with China's strategic expansionism. Hence, its interest is in ensuring that Asia remains multipolar and stable and its oceans and commons are run by liberal, transparent and multi-stakeholder regimes. The UK nods to this but needs to express its sentiment more strongly, and actively support Indian attempts in this direction.

More than wanting the UK to take on China in a zero-sum game, Modi's India will be asking the UK how it can contribute to India's own transformation and modernisation and the building of Indian capacities. Once this happens, a natural balance will be restored in Asia, to mutual benefit. The UK needs to recognise that it needs to be part of this process.

EMPATHY ON THE MOVEMENT OF PEOPLE

India formally embarked on the path of economic reform and globalisation later than most major economies—in 1991. This is now primarily driven by the talent of its people, as evidenced by the global success of Indian knowledge companies, and the ambition of its private sector. The biggest area of divergence between India and the UK is arguably in the sphere of immigration. While negotiating a prospective trade agreement, India will find it difficult to agree to liberalise terms of trade unless the UK shows greater imagination on opportunities for Indian professionals and students who have graduated from British universities.

From India's perspective, its stand looks perfectly justified as services account for two-thirds of its economy and any restrictions in the 'export' of these services is a blow on its economic growth. But looking at this same issue from the UK's point of view will force one to acknowledge that immigrant scepticism was a factor in the Brexit vote. From here, pulling up the drawbridges, or at least placing reasonable restrictions on foreign—and Indian—talent would seem like the safest political choice.

And India must accept that the UK is well within its rights to decide who can enter its borders, for how long and for what purpose. This is a sovereign right exercised by all nation-states, including India, and questioning this right will not lead to anywhere useful in this relationship. Yet, it is for British politics and politicians to find a compromise—not because India seeks it, but because the British economy itself needs to keep doors open for a certain type of global talent and to preserve its own idea of global values.

The UK's reluctance to pay heed to India's concerns on immigration is giving rise to an unhealthy impression in New Delhi and elsewhere in the country that London only wants India's business but not its talent. India's Commerce Minister Nirmala Sitharaman even made this point on an open platform to British Trade Secretary Dr Liam Fox during Prime Minister May's visit to India in November 2016.

Let me return here to Prime Minister Modi's reference to a 'Living Bridge' to emphasise that the foundations of the bilateral relationship have to go beyond trade or any immediate transactional necessity. A flow of people and the relationships they engender between the two nations generates a flow of ideas and helps build trust, which has to be the bedrock of any sustainable long-term relationship.

This is not to say that the UK does not have legitimate concerns on immigration. It quite emphatically does. And India must recognise these legitimate concerns—of the British government's right to know who is entering its borders—which the free-flowing EU immigration norms did not allow. There will need to be a period of adjustment, and India will need to give the UK some space to figure out the contours of a new workable immigration policy given that Brexit was essentially a vote against unchecked immigration from the EU.

But India will not wait forever. The letter written by forty-five Conservative MPs urging Her Majesty's government to bring in an easier visa regime for Commonwealth citizens could be a good starting point. The signatories, who include Sir Henry Bellingham, former foreign office minister, Tim Loughton, former education minister, and Shailesh Vara, former UK justice minister and chair of Conservative Friends of India, have written:

> The Prime Minister…made clear that post-Brexit Britain is open for business—not just with Europe but with the rest of the world as well. The Commonwealth includes five G20 countries, has a combined GDP of USD 10.4 trillion with annual GDP growth in excess of 4 per cent and offers a ready-made, English language trading network for Britain. We must be clear about the importance we place on our relationship with the Commonwealth and start the process of strengthening ties for crucial future trade negotiations. A key starting point in the renewal of our ties with our Commonwealth partners should be a reconfiguring of our border control system. Firstly, signs at border control that class every non-EU national as 'All other passports' should be changed to 'The Commonwealth and all other passports'. This is a small step but one that can be enacted quickly…'

FOR THE GREATEST COMMON GOOD

India is the world's sixth-largest economy and the UK the seventh. In keeping with the diplomatic tradition of both countries, the two governments should not only cooperate on matters of mutual interest and benefit but also pool their combined economic and political heft for the greatest good of the world.

It will not be the first time either country has taken up issues beyond their borders. In fact, it will be in keeping with the rich heritage of both. India and the UK can form special partnerships and work together on issues such as climate change, restructuring of the United Nations and the larger multilateral system to reflect contemporary realities rather than political considerations at the conclusion of World War II.

The UK and India have signed an agreement on participating in projects in third countries. Britain, for example, can help India's outreach in Africa. The UK has an existing footprint in that continent and serious developmental programmes. These can be leveraged. This is where a pooling of resources and intellectual capital between DFID and the Indian Ministry of External Affairs' Development Partnership Administration can create a force multiplier to attain higher social, economic, health and educational outcomes in Africa.

I have the privilege of serving on the advisory board of the Commonwealth Enterprise & Investment Council. From this vantage point, I can see tremendous opportunity to reimagine the Commonwealth—from a sleepy club of former colonies held together mainly by nostalgia to a vibrant trade and strategic bloc that straddles the globe and offers its members a real alternative to the EU, ASEAN and the proposed RCEP.

We should try to imagine a Commonwealth 2.0. I feel India should set the ball rolling by unilaterally offering to set up the Commonwealth's first business hub. The next Commonwealth Heads of Government Meeting or CHOGM, scheduled to be held in London in 2018 can be a defining moment in this proposed journey. If the Prime Ministers of both countries put their political heft behind this project, a win-win scenario can emerge for all fifty-two member countries.

Another area where India and the UK can combine forces for global benefit is cybersecurity. The UK has the cutting-edge innovation and India has the skilled human talent. These were the very conditions that made India so critical to meeting the Y2K challenge two decades ago. The emerging threats to cyberspace, to the internet and to the integrity of digital transactions and privacy can be met similarly.

An Equal-opportunity Partnership

London is India's preferred gateway to the world of international finance. And more than 800 Indian companies are present in the UK making them the third-largest foreign investor group in the UK and the second-largest job creators. The Tata Group is, in fact, Britain's largest manufacturer-employer. The attraction: Cultural similarities, familiarity with the British justice and legal system, easy assimilation of personnel into the host society and most importantly, unfettered access to the vast European common market.

These assumptions continue to hold but the last—arguably the most important consideration in business deals—could be turned on its head if Prime Minister May is unable to negotiate a good exit deal with Brussels. Most of these Indian companies have chosen the UK as the base of their European operations. Their fate—and those of the thousands they employ in Britain—is in balance.

It is natural that the changed ground realities will determine the future direction and paradigm of the relationship between London and New Delhi. In recent years, the UK has played a positive, if relatively reduced, role in India's economic development as New Delhi has looked at other potential partners such as the US, Japan, Germany and even China for investment and technology.

But after Brexit, India finds itself in the unfamiliar position of being in a relatively stronger position vis-à-vis the UK. With the US caught up in its own problems, western European democracies lining up behind Brussels and China taking the lead in building an alternative construct, New Delhi remains the only major global capital where the UK is likely to find both empathy and strategic alignment. The UK will need to take that extra step because India on its own is in the happy position of being wooed by many rival suitors.

Then again, a post-Brexit UK must consider the win-win potential in several tricky areas. For instance, medical tourism, which is currently constrained by restrictive EU norms. Can greater cooperation with countries like India provide the UK a viable working model to support its National Health Service? The economic logic is sound: It costs less than a fourth of the price an NHS patient would pay in Britain to get an open heart surgery done in India, and the success rates are world-class. But the emotional barrier will first need to be crossed by policymakers.

Openness by the UK to such 'out-of-the-box' suggestions (and there will be many) would be yet another signal to India that the UK is seeking a genuine partnership and not just one-way access into India's vast domestic market. Similar opportunities also exist in the market for the now massive Ayurvedic products industry, data management, legal and financial services. Given the unique confluence of events favouring closer economic ties, the time to seriously grapple the challenges and tap opportunities is now.

THE LIVING BRIDGE

The 1.5 million strong Indian diaspora in Britain has often been called its most influential minority, and with good reason. Highly educated and law abiding, they are successfully integrated at all levels of British society. I, like many other second-generation British Indians, was born to immigrant parents who came to the UK penniless from a troubled East Africa in the early 1970s. I was brought up in a council house and with State benefits in inner city Birmingham. But though I dismally fail Lord Tebbit's infamous 'cricket-test', through a combination of an increasingly open British society, and a sense of duty to do the very best for oneself and one's community (whatever their background), I can say without hesitation that Britain will be nothing other than home for me. I believe I speak for everyone I know of in my generation without exception.

Anyone who has had even a passing acquaintance with Britain's National Health Service will vouch for the dedication and quality of Indian doctors, many of whom have studied their basic medicine in India and completed their advanced specialisations in the UK. It is these doctors who ensure that the NHS remains a well run and affordable public health dispensing machine despite the many constraints that it faces.

Then, many members of the Indian diaspora have carved niches for themselves in British public life and contributed greatly to its success as a multicultural, multiracial society. Prime Minister Modi was the first to fully appreciate the importance of the Indian diaspora not only in the UK but in other nations as well, and has utilised their influence and goodwill to further India's diplomatic agenda. I had the privilege of leading the fabulous team that organised the 60,000 people reception for Prime Minister Modi at Wembley Stadium in November 2015. His unique connect with the UK's Indian diaspora was clearly visible, much to the awe of the then Prime Minister Cameron.

British politicians could take a leaf out of Prime Minister Modi's book and utilise the reach and influence of the Indian diaspora to enhance the substance of the bilateral relationship between the two countries rather than using them merely as a vote bank and political donors. Indeed, for all the complaints that Indians living in the UK have of it, the Indian High Commission in London does attempt to use the diaspora as a 'Living Bridge' and as a door opener to the British system. In contrast likewise, the Foreign and Commonwealth Office and the British High Commission in India must do much more to recognise the diplomatic value and utility of the UK's Indian diaspora.

It is time both my countries—I am of Indian origin but hold British citizenship—recognised and institutionalised the role of the Indian diaspora in the bilateral relationship matrix. The Indian diaspora in the UK can help the joint outreach I have proposed in preceding paragraphs, in Africa and the smaller Commonwealth countries, where the UK and India can cooperate not only on trade and strategic ties but also help local governments and communities build capacities in human development to enable them to lead better and more fulfilling lives.

Many, if not most British Indians trace their immediate origins to many of these countries and many, like me, retain strong cultural and business links with them.

A VOICE IN THE WILDERNESS

The old order is changing; a new one is not on the horizon. Look around and recall Rabindranath Tagore's words from 1927:

> *The world today is wild with the delirium of hatred,*
> *The conflicts are cruel and unceasing in anguish,*
> *Crooked are its paths, tangled its bonds of greed...*

These lines could just as easily have been written today and will remain relevant even a few years into the future. The post-World War II consensus that gave the world an unprecedented half a century of peace, prosperity and material well-being has broken down. No new consensus has emerged to fill the vacuum.

This is giving rise to unrest and war and global strife on a scale not seen since the first half of the previous century. I strongly feel the world should revisit the roots of civilisation when humankind first learnt that shared values and shared prosperity could lead to a better and more enlightened future than the rules of the jungle that privileged the might is right credo.

Every old civilisational idea needs to be revisited and repackaged to keep it relevant over the ages. Prime Minister Modi has taken two such ideas from the founding principles of Indian civilisational belief and coined the slogan *Sabka Saath, Sabka Vikas* (Development for all, discrimination against none) and also championed *Antyodaya*, which entails reaching out to the last person in the queue.

I think the time may now be ripe for taking these two ideas on to the world stage and to showcase to everyone that development need not be a zero sum game.

Call them by any other name if you don't like those coined by Prime Minister Modi but don't dilute the basic goals—any development mantra has to be able to make a positive contribution to the lives of the largest number of people to be successful. The idea of a global Britain can and should embody the same ideas, even if differently expressed.

But I fear that it won't be easy to disseminate these egalitarian ideas across the world for they will hurt too many special interest groups that currently draw authority and find sustenance from the asymmetry of power and prosperity that exists in the world. We, therefore, need to reimagine the way, for instance, news and views are disseminated across the world. Here, the BBC can help India and, perhaps, India can develop its own platform to propagate its views to the world. Unfortunately, progress towards this end is not even a work in progress. I hope this book will encourage at least some readers to move in the direction of creating a global voice which brings together the very best in talent and technology that this book advocates.

A Few Acknowledgements

I campaigned for the UK to remain in the EU and remain disappointed by the result, and also anxious about the long-term implications of Brexit. Yet, I recognise Brexit is an inevitability and while throwing challenges will also throw up opportunities. Rather than get dragged into the debate of what could have been and trying to re-run history, I felt that I should try to make a positive contribution in figuring out the UK's future outside of the EU, borrowing from the 'Living Bridge' vision of Prime Minister Modi.

Hence, the idea of a body of work that could be dipped into by policymakers, businesspersons, students and all those who want to make sense of how we can navigate our way through the cross-currents that seem to be hindering our progress. I also wanted to go behind the headlines to find the real nuggets of opportunity, without papering over the serious issues the UK and India will need to reconcile.

I express my sincere thanks and gratitude to all the contributors to this book who are not only eminent in their respective fields, but almost all whom I have known and worked with for many years. They have been true friends in their enthusiasm and support for this work. Thanks are also due to my friend Rajen Shah for the design of the book cover.

I thank my team and Arnab Mitra for helping me give shape to my thoughts whilst compiling this book, and Nomita Shah and Rajvi Singhvi, who have stayed with me through thick and thin over the years and all others who have helped me conceptualise and realise this book.

A final special word for my wife Dina, our daughters Avni and Anjali, and my parents and elder brother for their constant support and encouragement in all I do.

FOUNDATIONS
FOR THE FUTURE

Significant Bonds for the Twenty-first Century

Ambassador Ranjan Mathai

15 June 2015 was a clear day with brilliant sunshine over Runnymede, where a great throng had gathered in thousands, on the field which 800 years earlier had witnessed the signing of the Magna Carta, a foundation stone of the rule of law for the democratic world. After the Queen and the British prime minister inaugurated the commemorations of the anniversary of the Great Charter in a festive atmosphere, Princess Anne was led to a solemn event at the American Bar Association's memorial to the historic document. While walking up the path alongside a guard of honour towards the US visitors led by the US attorney general, she suddenly stopped, turned to the right, cut through the uniformed ranks and arrived at a shady tree. I was standing there with my wife to meet the Princess Royal, under the green canopy of leaves of the spreading Quercus robur which was a mere sapling in March 1994 when India's Prime Minister PV Narasimha Rao had planted it there. India's recognition of a landmark in the growth of human freedoms is unique, as the Indian prime minister was the only foreign leader to have made this gesture at that historic site. The royal visitor joined the other leaders, who have acknowledged the Indian presence on the field as reflecting the abiding bond of the commitment to democracy and rule of law between India and

Britain, a bond we both share with the USA. As PM Rao wrote, his tribute to the historic Magna Carta was 'an affirmation of the values of Freedom, Democracy and the Rule of Law which the people of India cherish and have enshrined in their Constitution'.

The understanding that we are ruled by consent is a critical element in the friendly ties between us as people and the ability of our leaders to empathise with each other's concerns, whether we are in agreement, or diverge when dealing with the issues of the day. I witnessed this during the meetings that two of India's prime ministers—Narendra Modi and Manmohan Singh—held with Prime Minister David Cameron and the closely-held discussions on the scourge of our times—terrorism. As India's foreign secretary, I was involved with dialogues with most of India's key partners and it was evident that with Britain we had a very special relationship, with strengths, as well as some limitations, that flowed from our domestic constraints. We were able, nevertheless, to share intelligence and build a most useful dialogue on counterterrorism taking account of our democratic frameworks. We have also gone beyond that in developing strategies for countering the related and equally serious challenges of extremism and radicalism. At Chequers, in November 2015, I was in the small group present when Prime Ministers Modi and Cameron spoke candidly on this theme; the two leaders then continued discussions privately while walking together on the grounds of the British PM's country house, with the warmth of their dialogue overcoming the chill of the crisp autumnal morning. An important outcome was the understanding that in the turbulent world we live in today, with politically-induced fervour and violence sometimes disguised as religious practice, India and Britain can work together to strengthen peace and civility in international discourse. Our traditions of even-handedness and following the middle path have resonance in the wider world.

Our constitutional foundations also make both India and Britain proponents of a rule-based world order. This is a valuable starting point for our relations in the future. Our global partnership, of course, evolved from a very different arrangement in an earlier era when India was bound into a global order created by the Pax Britannica in the nineteenth century. During this era, Indian trade and large Indian communities followed the British flag all around the world, and Indians became players in professional, legal, trading and sporting fraternities of a world, influenced, if not shaped, by British rules. Even as we threw off the shackles of British rule, these linkages enabled us to work in partnership as independent nations. For the future we have agreed to work in concert to maintain a rule-based world order; it is most useful that Britain recognises that this future world order will have to be one that evolves from our present, to reflect the changes in the world since the 1940s, when most of the structures of global governance were built. Britain supports expansion of the UN Security Council with India as a permanent member. We have both extended support to preservation of international maritime freedoms, and protection of other areas of the global commons. Similarly, we will work together in the G20 and other fora to reform international financial institutions, ensure greater fairness in world trade rules (including in regard to services and mobility of professionals), in the measures to tackle global warming, the management of the world's intellectual property regime and in the framing of regulations for the use of cyberspace.

We approach many issues of peace and security differently, but have many common interests in the Gulf, in the wider Indian Ocean Region and in Southeast Asia. In many parts of South Asia and along the Indian Ocean littoral areas of vital importance to India, Britain today, increasingly, finds that its own interests run parallel with those of India. India's geopolitical setting makes it a rim land power in Eurasia but one with strong heartland connections. It is no surprise that the dynamism of Prime Minister Modi's foreign policy flows out of the outward-looking tradition of his home state, Gujarat, which has been from ancient times a maritime centre of interest to the world, cited even in the first century CE Greek work *Periplus of the Erythraean Sea*. And Surat was indeed one of the earliest British maritime trading settlements in India. Britain and India have vital stakes in strengthening the maritime framework of global commerce and the blue economy, which have created prosperity and renewed opportunities in the world.

We both have interest in accelerating development processes in Africa and in the multilateral cooperation in the Commonwealth, which remains a unique grouping of countries of astonishing diversity bound by common values.

FROM BROOKE BOND TO THE MASALA BOND, WITH JAMES IN BETWEEN

The real test of a political relationship between nations is the evaluation of just how deeply it is rooted in the interests of their peoples. And the Indo-British relations meet the test fully.

Prime Minister Modi summed up a wide spectrum of these interests with a brilliantly evocative turn of phrase while addressing a crowd of 60,000 people at the Wembley Stadium during his visit to Britain in November 2015. He said that in the nineteenth century we spoke of Brooke Bond, in the twentieth, about James Bond, but the twenty-first century would be marked by the Masala Bond! This new financial instrument leverages the strengths of London's financial markets, to meet the burgeoning investment needs of India, particularly for infrastructure. The Prime Minister's public endorsement of the masala bonds highlights the perception that they present a win-win scenario, generating great financial opportunities for the UK, while speeding investments into the world's fastest-growing large economy, that is, India. They also extend the global role of the Indian Rupee. The bonds are only the latest feature of a vastly-increased range of forward-looking collaborative efforts between our institutions guided by the annual Economic and Financial Dialogue between India's finance minister and UK's chancellor of the Exchequer. The India–UK Financial Partnership has launched a variety of initiatives, including valuable inputs for India's bankruptcy law, for developing corporate bond markets in India, for leveraging of pension funds as investment vehicles and creation of a full-fledged reinsurance industry in India.

The closer financial ties we are building for the future are the revival in a new context of an old relationship. As PM Modi's remark recalled, the era of great British firms like Brooke Bond was built on Indian trade and Indian produce. After all, it was Indian trade and the Indian market that brought the British to India in the seventeenth century. What is less well known is that many of the economic and financial institutions created in Britain and globalised during the nineteenth century originated in the India trade. The activities and requirements of the East India Company had much to do with the growth of the City, the evolution of mechanisms like the interbank lending rate, global spread of bank branches and correspondents, the globalisation of insurance markets and so on. Mumbai and London, in particular, have been partners for centuries, and as India moves towards internationalisation of the Rupee, London may well be a launching pad....

It is well recognised in both countries that bilateral trade—both in goods and in services—has stagnated below its potential; trade figures show that for both of us the bilateral trade is less than 2 per cent of our global trade totals. However, we are, and will continue to be, major investors in each other's economies. Tata is Britain's largest manufacturing employer and BP is one of the most significant foreign investors in India. The rapid growth of India to the top league of the world's economies is now only a matter of time— and a short one at that in historical perspective. The Brexit decision sets Britain out on uncharted waters, as it leaves behind the European vocation in which it seemed settled over the last four decades. It will take more than the bravado of some Brexiteers—who seem to echo Shakespeare's 'come the three corners of the world in arms...and we will shock them'—to set a viable new course which ensures lasting security and prosperity for Britain. The UK's great strengths remain—in creative people, scientific advancement, research institutions, its financial sector, professional classes and communication skills. Its potential for developing energy and other resources could still surprise the world. As a major power with capable defence industries and worldwide interests, it could succeed, but would need international alternatives to the European anchor and trading hinterland it is now accustomed to. India is clearly a country where Britain could find opportunity, particularly if further European evolution leads to a revival of *L'Europe des Patries*. It bears recalling that in the 1960s before Britain joined the European Common Market, it absorbed 10 per cent of India's exports and supplied almost 25 per cent of India's manufactured imports. India was consistently an important supplier of goods to Britain, with a share of about 3 per cent of British imports even into the 1950s.

India is now embarked on a determined thrust for rapid economic growth, industrialisation and technological upgradation, greater integration with the world economy, building the skill sets of its 800 million young, and creating world-class infrastructure and transportation networks, and at the same time cleaning its rivers and more generally its physical environment.

It is set to become one of the leading powers of the world, and by aligning its capabilities with India's goals, Britain has a real opportunity. India had much to do with Britain's rise to global prominence in the past, and not just in finance and trade, but also in the provision of resources which extended Britain's reach. The oldest battleship afloat—once the pride of the Royal Navy—the HMS Trincomalee, which I went aboard in Hartlepool, was actually built in the early nineteenth century by the Wadias in Bombay! The Make in India programme, to which many British firms have responded positively, could provide the basis for a robust defence industrial partnership in the future. Our armed forces have many common traditions and apart from training together, have worked well as partners in international peacekeeping functions. It is fitting that the contribution of Indian soldiers to the British war efforts in both World Wars is now receiving proper recognition from historians, as well as the general public in both countries.

We in India are rightly proud of our ancient culture and heritage; it is only a matter of time before the idioms of Indian traditions and Indian languages regain worldwide currency. However we are, in some sense, and will remain, part of the English-speaking world, and this facilitates the task of communication between our peoples. Which is why the crowd at Wembley was both shaken and stirred to laughter at PM Modi's allusion to Bond, James Bond! This linguistic tie will provide the basis for increased collaboration in the creative industries which have great vitality in both India and Britain. It will also provide the platform for enhanced scientific and educational cooperation in the future. Indo-UK collaboration in science and technology has seen a major increase in investment over the last decade and has delivered significant benefits to both of us. Our young researchers are working together on cutting-edge technologies, solutions to great societal challenges and on the needs of our people in relation to health, energy and the environment. The UK–India Education and Research Initiative (UKIERI) is one of the most productive cooperative educational programmes between any two countries anywhere in the world.

While in London, I was often confronted with the issue of declining numbers of Indian students in the UK universities. As I worked closely with the British government and universities of the UK on the matter, I expect that the administrative structures of Britain would respond to the views of its universities on the value created by the flow of Indian talent into their halls of learning. Meanwhile the GIAN (Global Initiative of Academic Networks) programme, created at PM Modi's initiative, is expected to bring quality British (and other) academic expertise to the rapidly-expanding Indian university system, which would enable the latter to develop many more world-class institutions. Over time therefore, the Indian students in British universities are expected to be mainly in advanced courses of study or those studying in collaborative arrangements between Indian and British institutions. As high commissioner in London, I was also happy to assist in the promotion of Generation UK–India programmes launched in 2014, which will see thousands of young Britons undertake cultural immersion courses and work as teaching assistants in India. They will not stay as long as students completing multi-year degree courses, but will slightly redress the imbalance in the 300 to 1 ratio of students presently travelling from India to the UK and vice versa!

The closest, most popular link between India and the UK is in the field of sports, meaning specifically, cricket! (That is, if one excludes the realm of the spirits, with whisky cited as Britain's greatest gift to Indian tastes!) With the emergence of Indian spectators as the major power of the world's cricket audiences, the game of cricket has been more globalised than it ever was earlier.

This might well be a way to look at the future of India and UK as partners. The past has seen major shifts in the balance in our relationship. This will be true in the future as well, as the world adjusts to the rise of India. Recent developments suggest that Britain is well advanced on this trajectory and with sufficient political, business and cultural investments, our ties could become among the most significant in the twenty-first century world. That Theresa May chose India as the first country outside Europe to visit after becoming prime minister, is symbolic.

The Indian community in Britain constitutes the closest bond between us. The successful and well-integrated Indian community of over 1.6 million people ensures we remain permanently informed about and engaged with each other. I recall that when I met David Cameron for the first time in 2006, he seemed, in the mid-morning, still a trifle groggy; it was soon clarified that he had visited the house of a friend the previous night, and sat through many hours of a *Ram Katha* session along with friends from the community! This openness to other cultures is, as later election results demonstrated, good politics. But there is, as a result, an increasing intimacy of human interaction that weighs on Indo-British ties in ways that are difficult to replicate in other relationships. In the post-Brexit era, the influence of the Indian community in the UK is likely to grow even stronger. The Indian cultural traditions of yoga, holistic approaches to medicine, and balance in life, will come to weigh more than chicken tikka masala and Bollywood dance in the years to come!

India and Britain are headed for a new era in bilateral relations in which strengthening our friendly and profitable ties will be a matter of national consensus on both sides. We would be able to contribute to, and benefit from, the new trajectories on which both nations are set. We would remain key priorities for each other. In the years to come, the bonds between India and Britain would become critically important not just for each other, but in the world at large.

Ranjan Mathai is a former Foreign Secretary of India and former Indian High Commissioner to the UK.

Influencing Global Outcomes Together

Sir Michael Arthur

India is emerging as one of the small number of countries who will help determine the course of the twenty-first century. 'Our time has come, again,' is a refrain I hear regularly from Indian friends. They are right, of course. The world will be a better place if they maximise their influence. They probably won't, because the extraordinary complications flowing from India's rich diversity regularly lead India to achieve less than their plans and potential. There are significant exceptions to that gross exaggeration though, and one of the beauties of India is its ability to surprise.

Meanwhile, the UK is leaving the European Union and launching out on its own. It is rebalancing itself on a three-legged stool that will continue to comprise a leg called 'links to US/Canada'; one to the wider world; and one to continental Europe. It remains to be seen exactly how, and how successfully, that new stool will be made. As someone who felt perfectly comfortable on the pre-Brexit stool, with three stable legs, I am learning to adjust my balance. The risks of the change look more immediate and real than the opportunities. But let us see. India will need to be an important part of Britain's global leg— if India sees its interests that way.

So the three key questions are: Can the UK find success in its twenty-first century relationship with India? What does success look like? And can a huge twenty-first century India find value out of its links with the UK's global history and its ambitious, but very different global future? These questions are explored below.

The antecedents for this very real challenge were emerging even when I was high commissioner in the early years of the millennium. As the first ever high commissioner born since India's independence, I put much effort into trying to wake up the UK to the massive changes I saw starting to shape modern India. And in particular I pushed to forge links that would lead to a special relationship going forward into the twenty-first century.

The key was, and remains, to build on the strengths of our past while not allowing the undeniable sensitivities to get in the way of that future partnership.

Three little examples illustrate the point about the new direction of the relationship, not ignoring the past.

It was at that period that the Tata group decided to buy Jaguar Land Rover. What a symbolic historical turnaround! And what a success for both countries! The symbolism is just as powerful with Tata buying Corus Group, and now being deeply engaged with the UK government in how to bring that chapter to a positive conclusion in the face of wider global pressures.

Second, the British Council stimulated an extraordinary production of *A Midsummer's Night Dream* where there were actors—often actors and acrobats with only a simple street theatre training—who each spoke their own language. A dozen or so languages were used. The familiar plot and the action-packed storyline filled in the gaps. So successful was the India tour that it came back to London and ultimately to Stratford.

Third, in the year that Rolls Royce invested in a serious technology research centre in Bengaluru, I recall a fascinating seminar of top stem cell scientists taking place also in Bengaluru. To their amazement they found not only a depth of intellectual overlap in their research work, but also the added value of both working in countries where the legislative framework for permission on stem cell research was more similar than either side found anywhere else abroad.

Those examples are a long way from the type of bilateral relationship that prevailed during India's long period of extreme non-alignment. Or from the later complications that arose because of the UK's inevitably awkward position when India and Pakistan slogged out their differences over Kashmir.

India was changing fast when I arrived in 2003. Indian IT engineers had helped save the world from the catastrophe that we all anticipated with the millennium bug. India joined the UK in the rare club of being a nuclear weapon state, with all the responsibilities that it brings.

And as India increasingly focused on its competitive, and sometimes cooperative, relationship with China—which was to become a dominant driver of policy—we too focused on the India–China pairing. For example, on the fact that whereas China was a population of a billion who were demographically old, India's billion embraced more people under thirty-five than the entire population of Europe. How could we reach out to them? I was fascinated to find, as a British high commissioner, that the Indian Supreme Court occasionally cited precedents from the UK courts in the pre-Independence decades. With so many (and so distinguished) Indian lawyers of that generation having trained at the UK Bar, it is no surprise. That was a natural legal bond. But that link will mean nothing to the twenty-five year old woman accountant from Coimbatore. And she is India's future.

So, looking to the future, what are our common twenty-first century interests and what are the natural links that we can draw on to advance those interests?

India will be a central player in at least five of the most significant public policy issues of this century.

1. Global security and stability, starting in Asia but beyond.
2. Climate change—Helping to prevent deterioration and mitigating the consequences for the 1.3 billion people in India who are directly impacted by global warming.
3. Migration—Internal migration within India is a way of life and the flows are massive. India's existing diaspora is immense and immensely successful (40 per cent of Silicon Valley engineers are of Indian origin). Global mobility is going to accelerate, however much the OECD world tries to put up fences. India will inevitably be a major supplier. It also has almost unparalleled experience in managing mass migration.

4. Technological change—As we stand on the cusp of the next great IT and biotech revolutions, whatever they may be, I have no doubt that India will be one of the main players. From the Vedic mathematicians of 2,000 years ago onwards, Indians have mathematics in their DNA—who was it who invented place in number, the key to all subsequent mathematics?

5. Global trade—Although hitherto more of a closed economy than most large global countries, won't that have to change? India sits at the physical crossroads of much trade between Asia, Africa, Middle East and Europe. India needs to grow its economy in order to sustain, and feed, its burgeoning population. How India manages trade policy is still in flux. That it will become an even more central global player on trade policy issues must surely not be in doubt?

Seen through the UK end of that telescope those same challenges seem a little different:

Britain has for centuries been a leader beyond its size in contributing to global security, sometimes controversially so in certain regions, but preserving global security is a policy driver for the UK nonetheless. Today's priorities for the UK centre on Europe and NATO again. But India and the UK already have a deep relationship in the global fight against terrorism. They have common interests. These will grow, as both countries with global reach, value stability beyond their borders. We saw the beginnings of such cooperation over a decade ago in the joint work to combat fundamentalist terrorism, or to intercept pirates off Somalia.

On climate change, the two countries have diverged, sometimes fractiously. I had endless arguments about that with leading Indian experts a decade ago. But there are emerging points of common concern and bridges of corrective action. In a rational world, this fundamentally mutual long-term interest in managing climate change should lead us to much closer cooperation.

On migration, Britain currently sees its interests as being fundamentally opposed to India's ambitions to send more people to the UK, whether students, or business people, or just family link-ups (loosely defined!). This issue is going to need very careful managing in the decade ahead, lest its toxicity infect all the other areas where our two countries have so much potential together. The Indian diaspora in the UK—approaching 2 per cent of our population—is one of the anchoring strengths of our twenty-first century relationship. The UK must nurture and grow that bond, not fight it.

On technology, Britain too sees itself as one of the leading playgrounds and providers of expertise, as more breakthroughs come in bioscience, communications, computing and IT in the widest sense. The two countries have everything to gain from working together and building on their shared experiences. I fear that the toxicity of the migration challenge may get in the way of success in technology. There are ways to avoid that given there is mature political and non-polemical handling on both sides. But on this sensitive political issue, toxicity tends to triumph.

As for trade, well, the UK was the home of Adam Smith. His message has lost no force for modern generations in Britain, give or take the odd siren voice that can be managed. It is interesting that the trade policy pronouncements of, for example UKIP, are not as overtly protectionist as those of comparable populist movements in, say France. But the harsh reality is that India is not yet at a point where it is open to free trade access in the things that matter most to the UK—services like law and insurance and finance. Why else does Germany export so much more to India than the UK? Because India is prepared to allow more access for machine tools and other manufactured and consumer goods.

India can help both itself and the UK by a more open approach to economic issues. For example, London is one of the financial centres of the world, with a particularly global approach to finance. India's hugely successful global companies—of which there will be more, doing more—have a natural global partner in the city and all its globally competitive financial and legal services. The Indian political class does not yet see it that way.

As we look to a future where the two countries work together, globally, on these and other major areas, what are the positives that they can draw on that are distinctive to this relationship? I see several.

Language—It is always trumpeted as a leading positive link. True, but exaggerated. Most of the world now works in English. So this is no distinctive advantage. Only some 10 per cent of Indians actually have English language skills to the working level. But the link is there and language is fundamental to how people frame ideas. Leaders of both countries share that.

Law and all that goes with it—Our modern systems grew from the same plant. They have both evolved but the jurisprudence of the Indian Supreme Court is replete with references that would be equally recognisable in the British Supreme Court. I can think of no parallel between major countries anywhere else in the world that has the scale and depth of this legal bond.

Deep-seated commitment to pluralist democracy, and in the same tradition—By this I mean much more than just a common approach to parliamentary democracy, with the manifold overlaps between our two Parliaments that so intrigue people. We are of course, between us both, the oldest and the largest democracies. But beyond Parliament we both value a diverse, open and free press. We both have a strong culture of issue-based NGOs. We have strong traditions of public challenge over accountability. And so forth.

Education—The affinities between our two systems must seem extraordinary to an observer from a different tradition. The potential value of the bond is self-evident and immense. It is puzzling how successive governments seem incapable of taking this to the next level.

The UK Indian diaspora—It is a rich (in every sense!) link between us. With few other countries in the world does Britain share such depth and quality of diaspora. And similarly for India, the proportion of Indian-origin British nationals and their success in British society seem to me to be on at least a par, if not outweigh comparisons with the Indian-origin communities in the USA, Canada or Australia.

Affinities between the peoples of both countries—A shared love of, for example cricket, and the many gastronomic borrowings in both directions, attest to a very fundamental human link—fun and food. It is sad (and shameful!) that fewer Brits are as familiar with the Mahabharata as are Indians with Shakespeare. But there are many more British people who practice yoga than there are Indians who like walking dogs in the rain. On whisky we are about quits. The Indians beat the Brits on wedding glamour, but even British weddings today are a step change from the past—do we detect an Indian influence? And so it goes on.

All that leads to a fundamental mutual affection as long as the challenges of the present—especially those around migration issues—don't get in the way. These should be manageable with the right spirit.

My hopes rest with the young in both countries. They are far enough from the complex sensitivities of our shared past to see our common interests going forward. And their cultural likes and dislikes are far more shared than they were in the generation of my parents or even of me. They party the same way. They use social media the same way. They like each other's country for what it is.

But the real current test is for political and business leaders. When it comes to our fundamental national interests and ambitions, how can the other party help us? And will it? We have comparable goals. We know we can provide that reciprocal help. But it is easy to talk past each other. On both sides we have to recognise that a twenty-first century multilayered partnership is in the interests of us both. That won't happen without attention and effort at leadership level.

For me, success on this agenda would include the following (and more beyond):

- India and UK businesses enabled to cooperate globally on finance, law, insurance etc. Within both our countries and, together, beyond.
- Britain open to taking much more talent from India in our universities, start-ups, big businesses, the creative industries.
- A step change increase in foreign direct investment by each country in the other. Businesses will only make these decisions if the ambient economic culture is right—and better than now.
- India and the UK making common cause on both the technology opportunity and the policy requirement of combating global climate change.
- A closer strategic dialogue and cooperation on security issues in both Asia and Europe, with invigorated joint action to combat global terrorism and deeper links on the challenge of cybersecurity. These do not have to be visible as long as we are all confident they are happening.

All these should be win-win. Together we can have more influence on global outcomes than separately. At a time of changing US engagement in the world, this potential new era of UK–India cooperation takes on a new dimension.

So in both countries—the public sector, business and civil society alike—all have to recognise the potential of mutual engagement and support, and work to make it happen.

But the real novelty is my final question. We are equal partners. We have significant shared interests and can help each other achieve them. But do the majority of my fellow countrymen yet realise, who, in this twenty-first century partnership, needs who the most?

Sir Michael was Britain's High Commissioner to India between 2003 and 2007 and now works in the private sector, including as Director of an Indian-owned company.

ENHANCING STRATEGIC COLLABORATION

A Reformed United Nations—How India and the UK Must Collaborate

Ambassador Asoke Mukerji

In August 2017, India will mark the seventieth anniversary of its independence from the UK. This milestone follows the seventieth anniversary of the founding of the United Nations (UN) which was celebrated on 26 June 2015. The two events provide a useful framework to look at how India and the United Kingdom can collaborate in a reformed and dynamic UN. Their collaboration should build upon the foundations laid by the two countries in the UN over the past seventy years.

The UN itself was created as part of a process launched on 1 January 1942 in Washington DC by twenty-six allied nations fighting together in the Second World War. The 'Declaration by United Nations' document signed by these countries led to the negotiation and adoption of the UN Charter on 26 June 1945 in San Francisco.[1] Both the UK and India were among these 'original' members of the UN, whose membership did not require to be approved by the UN General Assembly (UNGA) on recommendation of the UN Security Council (UNSC).[2]

What are the areas in which India and the UK can cooperate in the framework of the UN in the twenty-first century? Two broad areas of such cooperation are contained in the UN Charter itself, which gives emphasis to issues of peace and security, as well as issues of socio-economic development and human rights. These two areas are interlinked, and both must be upheld if the peoples of the UN are to 'save succeeding generations from the scourge of war'.[3]

In the area of peace and security, the UN Charter gives 'primary responsibility' for the maintenance of international peace and security to the UNSC.[4] The UK, as one of the five permanent members of the UNSC since 1945, has wielded significant influence on issues placed on the Council's agenda. Though disappointed in the way in which its complaint of 1 January 1948, regarding armed aggression against its territory, was handled by the UNSC[5], India has supported UN peace initiatives as a necessary instrument to achieve the peaceful settlement of disputes.[6] India has consistently called for an inclusive dialogue process as the most sustainable way to bring about the peaceful settlement of disputes. This is rooted in the traditions of India's freedom movement, especially that of non-violence, to which Mahatma Gandhi, Martin Luther King and Nelson Mandela have contributed so powerfully in the twentieth century.

To provide substance to the UN's diplomacy, India has been the single-largest contributor, with 200,000 troops participating in forty-four out of the seventy-one UN peacekeeping missions mandated so far. Currently, UN peacekeeping is mired in controversies, both with regard to the policies of peacekeeping as well as the operations on the ground. This was brought out by the High-level Independent Panel on Peace Operations (HIPPO) set up by the UN Secretary General in 2015,[7] as well as by the statements of countries participating in the US-hosted Leaders' Summit on Peacekeeping in September 2015.[8]

Concerns have been expressed regarding the ineffectiveness of UN peacekeeping operations, especially in protecting civilians, including women and children caught up in armed conflicts. Cooperation between India and the UK in the future evolution of UN peacekeeping is a practical way for ensuring the effectiveness of UN peacekeeping operations, based on the three traditional principles of 'consent of the parties, impartiality and the non-use of force except in self-defence or defence of the mandate'.[9]

India and the UK have a shared interest in ensuring that such concerns are properly addressed by the UNSC. The UK, which is the driving force (or 'penholder') for peacekeeping issues in the UNSC,[10] should take the initiative and ensure that interested troop-contributing countries, like India, which are not represented in the UNSC, 'participate in the decisions of the Security Council' concerning the deployment of their UN peacekeepers.[11] So far, India has not participated in such direct decision-making of the UNSC, except when it has been a member of the UNSC in a non-permanent capacity.[12]

A significant area where India and the UK must collaborate more actively to create a more dynamic and responsive UN is in the reform of the Security Council itself. Both countries were part of the consensus decision by world leaders at the 2005 UN World Summit calling for these reforms,[13] considered necessary to make the UNSC more effective and representative of the contemporary world. In September 2015, India and the UK, together with 120 other UN member states, successfully tabled a text in the UNGA on which negotiations for reforming the UNSC could take place.[14] The UK has publicly expressed its 'commitment to a reformed UNSC with India as a permanent member'.[15]

How can this happen? As a permanent member, the UK should undertake a diplomatic initiative to get the consensus of the other four permanent members of the UNSC to accepting expansion in both permanent and non-permanent categories of the UNSC. Only after additional permanent seats in the UNSC are created by the UNGA as a result of text-based negotiations will India be able to harvest the support of the UK and its other international partners in its campaign to be elected a permanent member of the UNSC.

Closely integrated with international peace and security, and impacting directly on socio-economic development and human rights, is the response of the UN to terrorism. India and the UK have shared concerns on countering terrorism emanating from Pakistan, whether in the case of the 7 July 2005 London bombings,[16] or the 26 November 2008 terror attacks in Mumbai, in which 164 innocent civilians, including one UK national, were killed, and 308 persons injured, by the Pakistan-based terrorist group, Lashkar-e-Taiba (LeT).[17] Leaders of India and the UK have 'reiterated their call for Pakistan to bring the perpetrators of the November 2008 terrorist attack in Mumbai to justice.'[18]

Using international law as codified by the UNGA to prosecute or extradite terrorists, a principle upheld by the International Court of Justice,[19] should be a common commitment for both India and the UK. A tangible outcome of India–UK cooperation in this area would be the early conclusion of a Comprehensive Convention on International Terrorism (CCIT). The first draft of the CCIT was proposed by India two decades ago in the UNGA. The UK and India should now collaborate with other like-minded countries to move the latest draft text of the CCIT prepared by the chairman of the Ad Hoc Working Group for adoption by the UNGA.[20] This will send a strong signal about the seriousness of India–UK collaboration on peace and security issues.

According to the UNHCR, 65 million people are currently displaced by war and persecution. This is the highest such number since the Second World War when the UN was founded.[21] This mammoth human crisis has the potential to trigger off global instability.

If the UN is to succeed in warding off this impending crisis, it has to act quickly to implement the long overdue reforms of the UNSC, and accelerate its ambitious Agenda 2030 for sustainable development. The agenda was adopted by world leaders at the special summit of the UNGA in September 2015. India and the UK collaborated closely on identifying and negotiating the adoption of the agenda, which has the seventeen sustainable development goals (SDGs) at its core.[22]

The platform for conceptualising the SDGs and tracking their implementation is the UN Economic and Social Council, or ECOSOC.[23] During the India–UK Summit held in November 2015, the 'two Prime Ministers welcomed the adoption of the Post-2015 Development Agenda "Transforming our World: The 2030 Agenda for Sustainable Development" and committed to supporting its implementation. They recognised that the new 2030 Agenda along with the sustainable development goals has poverty eradication as its overarching focus.'[24]

Areas for mutually-beneficial cooperation between India and the UK within the framework of the UN's Agenda 2030 have already begun to be prioritised. For example, India and the UK committed themselves to increased cooperation in the field of health. Under their existing memorandum of cooperation, the two countries have ongoing projects in 'areas including medical education and training, universal health coverage, containment of anti-microbial resistance (AMR), improving patient safety through quality, safe and efficacious drugs and the collaboration between NICE International, UK and the Department of Health Research in India on medical technology assessment.'[25] This cooperation feeds into the mutual implementation of the objectives of SDG 3, devoted to 'Good Health and Well-being."

Similarly with regard to India–UK cooperation in education, which has been quantified by the joint statement to include the 'UK's plans to send 100 academics to India over the next two academic years as part of the Global Initiative for Academics Network (GIAN); and the ambition for 25,000 UK students to come to India through the Generation UK–India programme by 2020, including 1,000 UK interns with Tata Consultancy Services in India by 2020.'[26] Such initiatives will significantly help implement SDG 4 on 'Quality Education'.

Special priority has been given by India and the UK to the development of smart and sustainable cities in India with UK collaboration, as well as the 'Thames/Ganga partnership' for healthy river systems.[27] These activities will directly feed into the implementation of the SDG 6 on 'Clean Water and Sanitation' and SDG 11 on 'Sustainable Cities and Communities'.

A common commitment to tackling the challenge of climate change has brought India and the UK together. In a joint statement issued during the visit of Prime Minister Narendra Modi to the UK in November 2015, the two sides 'stressed that addressing climate change and promoting secure, affordable and sustainable supplies of energy are shared strategic priorities for India and the UK.' A special focus of India–UK cooperation will be on environmentally friendly technology. The joint statement reiterated the commitment of both countries to 'foster innovation and research and development to make clean energy more affordable.'[28]

India–UK cooperation under this initiative will expedite the achievement of targets under the SDG 7 on 'Affordable and Clean Energy' as well as the objectives of the SDG 13 on 'Climate Action'.

India and the UK can collaborate together to meet targets under SDG 8 on 'Decent Work and Economic Growth', following up on the UK Prime

Minister Theresa May's statement that 'no G20 country has invested more in India since the turn of the century than Britain, while India is Britain's second-biggest jobs creator.'[29]

India–UK collaboration on infrastructure has been identified as a priority area with implications for India's sustainable growth. During the India–UK Summit in November 2015, the two countries recognised the importance of 'a long-term strategic partnership between India and the UK on the former's flagship infrastructure investment initiative, the National Investment and Infrastructure Fund (NIIF), and announced the setting up of an India–UK partnership fund under the umbrella of the NIIF. The collaboration will help bring global investors through the City of London to help finance Indian infrastructure in a sustainable way, further supporting India's rapid growth.'[30] In turn, this collaboration will help implement the achievement of the SDG 9 on 'Industry, Innovation and Infrastructure'.

An interesting new area for bilateral India–UK cooperation within the UN framework is with regard to the UN's SDG 12 on 'Responsible Consumption and Production'. Both India and the UK co-sponsored the historic UNGA resolution of 2014 declaring the International Yoga Day.[31] When Prime Minister Narendra Modi proposed this Day in his maiden address at the UNGA in September 2014, he had pointed out that, 'We can achieve the same level of development, prosperity and well-being without necessarily going down the path of reckless consumption.'[32]

Before looking at the future prospects for India–UK collaboration in a reformed and dynamic UN, it would be useful to emphasise the unique role that the two countries have carved out for themselves in addressing issues of the digital era, where information and communication technology (ICT) plays a major role. The Cyber Dialogue between India and the UK was launched in 2012,[33] and covers the key areas of the digital commons, such as tackling cybercrime, promoting cybersecurity, skill development, strengthening of digital infrastructure and cooperation within the UN on the development of international norms of behaviour for cyberspace. This was emphasised during the India–UK Summit in November 2015.

As two significant 'knowledge societies', collaboration between India and the UK will be of positive benefit for the UN's ambitious programme of using

ICT for accelerating development under the Tunis Agenda and aligning this activity with the implementation of Agenda 2030.[34]

In conclusion, this review of the prospects for India–UK collaboration in the context of a reformed and dynamic UN will not be complete without a reference to the implications of the June 2016 referendum (Brexit) in the UK, which resulted in a vote to leave the European Union (EU).[35] India's relations with the UK predate its relations with the EU. However, ever since the UK joined the EEC in 1973 and subsequently became part of the EU's Treaty of Lisbon of 2010, India's interaction with the UK has been enhanced by the UK's role in Europe. Nowhere is this more evident than in the decisions of Indian businesses to invest and locate their activities in the UK, which for many Indian companies are their European headquarters.

Apart from its impact on relations between India and the UK, and India and the EU, the June 2016 referendum will also impact on many of the issues mentioned above in the context of India–UK collaboration in the UN. After all, two major EU members (the UK and France) are currently permanent members of the UNSC, while another major EU country, Germany is a declared aspirant for permanent membership of a reformed Security Council. Only after the negotiations between the UK and EU conclude will the extent and directions of these consequences be known.

Asoke Mukerji was India's Permanent Representative to the United Nations.

ENDNOTES

1. The signature pages of the UN Charter contain an interesting fact relating to India. The UN Charter was signed by two Indian representatives—one for British India, represented by the Indian politician Sir Ramaswami Mudaliar of the Justice Party, who was a Member of the War Cabinet, and the other for the 560 Princely States of India, represented by Sir VT Krishnamachari, who had been Prime Minister of the Princely State of Baroda between 1927 and 1944.
2. *Charter of the United Nations*, Articles 3 and 4. Published by the United Nations Department of Public Information. Available at http://www.un.org/en/charter-united-nations/
3. Ibid., Preamble.
4. Ibid., Article 24.1 of the UN Charter.
5. Dasgupta, C. *War and Diplomacy in Kashmir, 1947-48*. Published by Sage Publishers, India. https://in.sagepub.com/en-in/sas/war-and-diplomacy-in-kashmir-1947-48/book243763
6. An entire Chapter of the UN Charter, Chapter VI (which precedes authorisation of the use of armed force as an exception in Chapter VII), is devoted to the peaceful settlement of disputes. *Charter of the United Nations*. Published by the United Nations Department of Public Information. Available at http://www.un.org/en/charter-united-nations/

7. HIPPO Report, UN Document No. A/70/95–S/2015/446*. Available at http://www.un.org/en/ga/search/view_doc.asp?symbol=S/2015/446

8. The Leaders' Summit, New York, September 2015. For further details see http://www.un.org/en/peacekeeping/operations/leadersummit.html

9. UN Document No. A/70/95–S/2015/446* dated 17 June 2015, containing the Report of the High-level Independent Panel on Peace Operations (HIPPO). Page 46, paragraph 124. Available at http://www.un.org/en/ga/search/view_doc.asp?symbol=S/2015/446

10. For a listing of 'pen-holders' in the UNSC, see 'Chairs of Subsidiary Bodies and Pen-holders for 2016' published by Security Council Report. Available at http://www.securitycouncilreport.org/un-security-council-working-methods/atf/cf/%7B65BFCF9B-6D27-4E9C-8CD3-CF6E4FF96FF9%7D/Penholders%20and%20Chairs.pdf

11. *Charter of the United Nations*, Article 44. Published by the United Nations Department of Public Information. Available at http://www.un.org/en/charter-united-nations/

12. India has been represented in the UNSC as a non-permanent member seven times since 1945, most recently in 2011-2012.

13. 2005 World Summit Outcome, paras. 153-154, contained in UN Document A/RES/60/1 dated 24 October 2005. Available at https://documents-dds-ny.un.org/doc/UNDOC/GEN/N05/487/60/PDF/N0548760.pdf?OpenElement

14. The text was part of UNGA Decision 69/---. Available at the United Nations website at http://www.un.org/en/ga/president/69/pdf/letters/050515_security-council-reform-framework-document.pdf

15. Joint Statement on the United Kingdom–India Summit, 2015. Available at https://www.gov.uk/government/news/joint-statement-on-the-united-kingdom-india-summit-2015

16. See 7/7 London Bombings. Available at http://www.history.co.uk/study-topics/history-of-london/77-london-bombings

17. See a full account of the Mumbai Terror Attack at https://fas.org/irp/eprint/mumbai.pdf

18. Ibid.

19. The Habre Case. See International Court of Justice Docket available at http://www.icj-cij.org/docket/files/144/17084.pdf

20. See UN Doc. A/68/37 dated 15 May 2013, issued in Official Records of 68 UNGA, Supplement No. 37. The text is given in Annex I, pages 5-14.

21. Global Trends 2015 Report issued by UN High Commissioner for Refugees. Available at http://www.un.org/apps/news/story.asp?NewsID=54269#.WCWzHfl96M8

22. The text of Agenda 2030 and the 17 Sustainable Development Goals are available at the UN Website. See https://sustainabledevelopment.un.org/content/documents/21252030%20Agenda%20for%20Sustainable%20Development%20web.pdf

23. *Charter of the United Nations*, Chapter X, Articles 61-72. Published by the United Nations Department of Public Information. Available at http://www.un.org/en/charter-united-nations/. India was elected the first President of the ECOSOC when it met in London's Central Hall in 1946. Since then, India has played a prominent and pioneering role in advocating human rights and socio-economic issues, including racial discrimination (subsequently apartheid) in South Africa, war crimes and genocide, gender parity, the rights of children, as well as environmental protection and sustainable development, linking environment and development in a holistic relationship.

24. Joint Statement on the United Kingdom–India Summit, 2015. Available at https://www.gov.uk/government/news/joint-statement-on-the-united-kingdom-india-summit-2015

25. Ibid.

26. Ibid.

27. Ibid.

28. India–UK Joint Statement on Energy and Climate Change, November 2015, London. Available at https://www.gov.uk/government/uploads/system/uploads/attachment_data/file/476689/India–UK_Joint_Statement_on_energy_and_climate_change.pdf

29. Bangalore reception for the India–UK Tech Summit: Prime Minister's Speech, available at https://www.gov.uk/government/speeches/bangalore-reception-for-the-india-uk-tech-summit-prime-ministers-speech

30. Joint Statement on the United Kingdom–India Summit, 2015. Available at https://www.gov.uk/government/news/joint-statement-on-the-united-kingdom-india-summit-2015

31. Resolution No. A/RES/69/131 dated 11 December 2014 adopted by the UNGA on 'International Day of Yoga'. Available at http://www.un.org/en/ga/search/view_doc.asp?symbol=A/RES/69/131

32. English rendering of the PM's statement at the general debate of the 69th session of the United Nations General Assembly (UNGA). Available at http://www.pmindia.gov.in/en/news_updates/english-rendering-of-the-pms-statement-at-the-general-debate-of-the-69th-session-of-the-united-nations-general-assembly-unga/

33. Joint Statement on Cooperation between India and the UK on Cyber Issues, November 2012. Available at http://www.mea.gov.in/bilateral-documents.htm?dtl/20792/Joint+Statement+on+Cooperation+between+India+and+the+United+Kingdom+on+Cyber+Issues

34. UNGA Resolution A/RES/70/125 dated 1 February 2016. Available at http://unctad.org/en/PublicationsLibrary/ares70d125_en.pdf

35. See a roundup on the Brexit referendum by the BBC on 10 November 2016. Available at http://www.bbc.com/news/uk-politics-32810887

Trading Places: India and the UK Can Nuance Transactional Globalisation

Ashok Malik

O n Wednesday, 29 March, the United Kingdom formally invoked Article 50 of the Treaty of Lisbon and began the process of withdrawing from the European Union (EU). This narrative will culminate in the summer of 2019, when the UK will cease to remain a member of the EU. The precise nature of the relationship between the UK and the EU following that— and following the full realisation of the aspirations and wishes of the Brexit referendum of 2016—remain unclear. Will the UK still have access to the European common market even if domestic public opinion no longer permits it to allow free movement to EU workers? Is the mood in Brussels, where the fabled and yet infamous EU bureaucracy is located, one for 'negotiating' with the UK or 'punishing' it? These are questions that remain unanswered.

What is both logical and apparent is that there are limits to which the principal powers of the EU—Germany and France—can go to accommodate the UK following its withdrawal from the European compact. A hardnosed punter would tilt in favour of a 'hard Brexit' outcome than any other alternative. To allow a special dispensation for the UK, one that grants it the equivalent of current trading rights with the EU for goods and services but places restrictions on labour, would simply not be feasible unless the

EU is willing to countenance similar demands from other countries and fundamentally renegotiate the basis of the EU itself.

It follows then that a post-2019, post-EU Britain would require new friends, new trading partners, new international anchors and new safe harbours—as a global power that is geographically just off the mainland of Europe but retains an economic and political profile independent of the continent. Failure to achieve this could mean irrelevance. For the UK, to make a success of its post-Brexit future is not merely an option—it is an imperative. In this, its relationship with old allies—the transatlantic bonds with the United States and the traditional white dominions of the Commonwealth such as Canada and Australia—as well as its search for partnerships with emerging powers such as China and India acquire a greater urgency.

The 'India question' is a tantalising one. For the UK, a post-2019 trade arrangement—in a dream scenario, a free trade agreement—with India seems desirable and a low-hanging fruit. History and nostalgia and strong business-to-business and people-to-people ties would suggest that. Behind that appealing façade, though, there lies a gamut of challenges. If these are left unaddressed, the potential of the India–UK friendship will never be fully realised. The past is no guarantor of success in the future; sometimes it is at the very root of the problem, or of an appreciation of the problem.

ONE IN THE INDIA CROWD

Till the mid-1990s, the British high commission was the default repository of wisdom in New Delhi's diplomatic enclave. It was widely recognised as the embassy with the best connections in and institutional knowledge of India. Part of this was legacy, flowing from years of British engagement with India well before the country's independence in 1947. This had given British officials and interlocutors a certain familiarity with Indian systems.

Some of it had to do with personal affinities, including between British officials and two generations of post-1947 Indian civil servants and political and business elites being educated in the UK. Complemented by a natural curiosity that is the stock-in-trade of any good diplomat, this gave Britain unusual expertise in everything from Indian military purchases to the intricacies of a state election. Other governments in the West deferred to British insight and knowledge about India.

Over the past twenty years, this landscape has changed dramatically. As India's economic and trade links as well as its political ambitions have grown, so has its exploration for international partners. In an expanded and wider canvas, the UK has found itself crowded out. Since the Pokhran nuclear tests of 1998, the United States and India have embarked on building a robust partnership. Other countries in the West—used here as both a geographical and political expression—such as Germany, Israel, Singapore and Australia have also solidified relations with the Indian government, with individual states, with a variety of stakeholders in business and civil society.

Consequently, embassies or high commissions of each of these countries can today match, sometimes better, British expertise on the state of play in India. As a business partner or technology reference point too, Britain now competes and often takes second place to many others, or is lost in the crowded room with the EU. When India seeks political associations on one of so many international platforms, whether climate change mitigation talks or at the Nuclear Suppliers Group, the UK is far from a default or sometimes even a natural partner. This is the hard reality.

Ambition Beyond Transactionalism

Where does this leave the UK? Amid goodwill and a lingering familiarity, it finds itself jostling for a role in a new India. The new India too wonders what to make of the UK, other than the preference for London as a holiday destination or, for the seriously rich Indian, the location of a second home, in the heart of the Western world.

On paper and in practice, a whole range of shared concerns unite the two nations: Cybersecurity, green technology, intelligence sharing and assessments of the risks of terrorism from the broader Pakistan region and the greater Middle East, the stated quest for a wider trade and investment relationship, the agreement on an international architecture—whether for internet governance or the Indian Ocean—that is founded on liberal and democratic principles, rather than angular ideas that a Moscow or a Beijing may have.

In theory, a marriage of British technology and Make in India—the endeavour to raise the share of manufacturing from the current 17 per cent of GDP to 25 per cent of (a much bigger) GDP by 2025—can work well in areas as far apart as military hardware, aerospace and pharmaceuticals.

In theory, as Indian students seek admission to universities across the planet—from Australia to the United Arab Emirates (UAE), Germany to the US—it makes little sense that numbers to the UK are falling. Perhaps that is only a temporary blip that the declining pound will take care of, or will it?

In theory, India should open its economy to British legal and related services firms, as well as lower tariffs for British whiskies. The former will employ young Indian graduates in any case, and the latter will ultimately benefit the Indian consumer. In theory, as co-leaders of the Commonwealth—a twentieth century relic institution that can only be relevant to the twenty-first century if New Delhi embraces and invigorates it—India and the UK should be able to pool their impressive individual developmental and assistance programmes in Africa to make a bigger impact and balance the influence of China.

Nevertheless, in the minutiae and transactionalism of this wish list, what is missing is ambition. Little of this amounts to a transformational re-imagination of British and India relations. Rather, it prioritises the petty give-and-take, the careful and niggardly negotiation in the manner of a trade deal, or, given the rate of progress in these matters, the negotiation over the parameters of negotiating a trade deal: A Nation of Shopkeepers talking to a Civilisation of Bargain Hunters.

Can India and the UK move beyond these clichés? Brexit offers a potential inflection point for not just London's engagement with the rest of the British Isles but also for their collective dynamic with India.

Of course, there is always the possibility that enthusiasm on either side could fall even further. After all, absent of access to the common European market and with the prospect of a 'hard Brexit', the UK could find itself less alluring for Indian companies seeking a beachhead in the West or at the gates of Europe. That apart, suspicion of and discomfort with migration was an undeniable theme of the Brexit campaign. It wasn't the only strand that was up for discussion in the summer of 2016, as British voters prepared for the referendum, but it was definitely part of the mix.

To Indians, it seemed a puzzling issue on which to be put on the defensive. What has continued to astonish wider public opinion in India is the inability of ordinary people, political polemicists and sometimes even covenants and statutes to distinguish between refugees and asylum seekers, white-collar expatriate workers who add value to a modern economy, and fee-paying students who contribute to one of the UK's biggest exports (education services) and seek a temporary, perhaps two-year, working visa concession on graduation.

Could such niggles be ironed out? India believes they can, but in doing so also makes an assumption on the underpinnings of British nationhood and the urges behind Brexit. Its bets on a less European but more globalised UK—on Great Britain's enlightenment trumping Little England's anxieties.

THE FUTURE ISN'T IN NOSTALGIA

The EU as an entity has tended to bewilder Indian government officials. Dealing with the Brussels bureaucracy, rather than with political leaderships rooted in and answerable to domestic constituencies, has been problematic and contributed to the delay in concluding an India–EU FTA. The fault is not entirely that of the EU; Indian trade negotiators must take a fair share of the blame. Having said that, on issues such as textile quotas, market access for Indian fruits and food products and data privacy laws for IT companies, India has found the EU unduly protectionist and its negotiators more ideological than transactional.

As a result, India has better bilateral relations with key EU countries— Germany, France, even Poland and Hungary for that matter—than with the EU as a whole. In parallel, India sees Brexit not as a protectionist mechanism but as an opportunity for Britain to break out of the restrictive, and to India's mind protectionist, trade regimes and practices of the EU. In an ideal realisation, it could lead to a UK that far from shunning global economic currents only calls for some incorporation of genuine British voter concerns, and envisages greater deregulation, in the financial markets and services sector in particular, in the medium term. This proposition would present London as a European Singapore: A shining city, free of the EU but still the financial capital of the world.

That is India's hope, for it would offer India and a number of Indian stakeholders room for a meaningful and mutually enriching arrangement with British counterparts. However, it needs to be said that this interpretation of a post-2019 UK is far from unanimous in Britain itself and requires a degree of honest conversation between British political and business leaders and voters in the period ahead. A conversation with India is only feasible after a conversation within Britain itself—a conversation in which Britain recognises what the implications of Brexit can and cannot be and why the past, comforting as it is in its certainties, is not always the best instrument to navigate the future.

Nostalgia is a powerful force. In the aftermath of a referendum summer of high emotion, British politicians have found it difficult to just walk away from it. One expects as the negotiations with Brussels proceed, as tempers rise, nostalgia and national pride will once more emerge as powerful social phenomena, especially as ordinary Britons struggle to make sense of a society in flux. At a conference in Greece a few weeks after the Brexit vote, this writer heard an elderly British politician extol the decision to leave the EU and said it was time 'to get the factories of northern England humming again'. That was obviously a case of hope and nostalgia overrunning economic logic, rationalism and reality, but in a democracy one cannot wish these away.

Nostalgia shaped the terms of the referendum of 2016. In a sense, the Brexit vote was not a rejection of globalisation, but a debate on the terms and models of globalisation. Globalisation is always acceptable if it leaves you and your country better off. Take an example. When the Brexit referendum took place, one million citizens of Commonwealth countries who are residents of the UK voted. This group, which included many Indians, is not to be confused with British citizens of Commonwealth origin. It has the right to vote in British elections under anachronistic rules going back to an imperial age.

On the other hand, three million citizens of other EU countries who were also resident in Britain were not allowed to vote. As such, more than de-globalisation, the Brexit referendum was a contest between older and newer templates of globalisation, the older template being forged by memory and nostalgia.

GLOBALISATION WITH A NATIONAL FACE

We live in an age when context may be no older than a Twitter timeline and when instant punditry could appear seductive and tempting in its offering of quick conclusions and false equivalences. There is the facile view, for instance, that three major democracies—the US, the UK and India—are in the throes of a very similar predicament. They are all run by right-wing governments, or at least centre-right political persuasions. All of them recently concluded elections—in the case of the UK, a referendum—where issues of national identity and/or ethnicity seemed to have a certain salience.

All three are in their own manner reassessing their approach to the liberal trading order and making an appraisal of the gains and losses of two decades of globalisation: Of ten years of FTAs (India), twenty years since the founding of the World Trade Organisation (the US) and twenty-five years since the Treaty of Maastricht (the UK). International economic volatility, subdued growth and demand, and the hunger for jobs at home are influencing politics and policymaking in New Delhi, London and Washington DC, alike.

Even so, there is a crucial difference. Globalisation and economic openness are hardwired into the Indian and British systems. Indeed, these are cultural and civilisational characteristics for both peoples. Over millennia, India, with its territorial and maritime boundaries merging into the great trading routes of the world, has known no other way. Over centuries, Britain, surrounded by the seas, an obscure island off the northern coast of Europe, has known no other way. For them, trade has been destiny. The US, behind the twin moats of the Atlantic and Pacific, has episodically known other ways.

That is why the Trump mandate in the heartland of America has protectionist impulses that, frankly, Brexit does not have and cannot sustain. Likewise, the Narendra Modi government's Make in India endeavour is as much a means to leverage India's market for local value creation as to link India to global supply chains. This need not be the collaborative route America's current administration will take. India and the UK are still more invested in the international trading regime, albeit they recognise domestic and democratic pressures would force them into a transactional globalisation, rather than towards ultimately unviable if maximalist free-trade idealism.

On a nuanced understanding of the obligations and limits of the liberal democratic order in the international system, and a shared responsibility on issues as diverse as climate change and the global developmental agenda, India and the UK will find more in common with each other than with contemporary America; and New Delhi and London may find it useful to cooperate in trying to leaven and moderate Washington DC's instincts.

This moment of disruption in the world system is not without its ironies.

300 years ago, as Europe began its expansionist phase, the great powers of the continent sought colonies and Trucial or vassal states in Asia, the Middle East and Africa. Today, that journey is taking place in the reverse direction. As they outgrow their immediate neighbourhood and develop transcontinental aspirations and linkages, the new powers of Asia are searching for base stations in Europe and the West. Abu Dhabi, the leader of the UAE, has invested heavily if controversially in Serbia. China, using Macau as a doorway, has built a special relationship with Portugal.

Can India and the UK do something similar? India lacks the massive sovereign wealth funds of Abu Dhabi and the UAE, as also the single-minded determination of the Chinese state. It makes up with its strengths as an open, creative and entrepreneurial society. The UK, on the other hand, is a more complex, more capable and much larger actor—a permanent member of the Security Council, Brexit or no Brexit—and with deeper institutional and diplomatic capacities than a Serbia or a Portugal or a relatively minor European nation that would easily slip into a subsidiary alliance. Most tellingly, both India and the UK can never be anything but democracies—that makes them a natural fit but also testy negotiators.

Having said that, India recognises that Britain is its natural harbour in the West. That is why a post-Brexit special relationship, with implications for trade as well as politics, carries such political weight in New Delhi. That spirit of accommodation needs to be apparent in London as well, if only to allay the Indian concern that Britain's interest in 'talks about trade talks' is genuine and not geared towards merely getting a better deal from Brussels. For the coming two years, India and the UK will argue, bitterly and separately. At the end of those two years, it is for them to demonstrate that they can make music together.

Ashok Malik is a leading Indian political columnist and distinguished fellow at the Observer Research Foundation, New Delhi.

India and the Commonwealth— Opportunity to Set a Dynamic New Agenda

Lord Jonathan Marland

One of the most notable elements of the India–UK relationship in recent years is the complete absence of the Commonwealth in our bilateral discourse. We quite rightly talk about the values we share—values of democracy, responsibility, the rule of law and fair play—yet, we never speak about them through the lens of the Commonwealth, the network that both countries played key roles in establishing and that also promotes these values across the fifty-two member states.

Back in late 2015, during Prime Minister Narendra Modi's visit to the UK, then Prime Minister David Cameron explained his fear that the relationship between Britain and India had for some years been imprisoned by the past. In her first visit to India in 2016, and first bilateral foreign trip outside of Europe, Theresa May also stressed that she wanted to talk about the importance of the relationship today and in the future, not to be tempted to look to the past and to take for granted or make assumptions about the links that we have. But she went on to say that 'we stand the greatest chance of success when we work with partners with whom we share similar values, legal systems, approaches to business and ways of looking at the world.'

Perhaps then, it is the Commonwealth's association with the past that has cut it out of current dialogue—a perceived anachronism that is no longer a relevant part of the new relationship between our two countries. However, as I have consistently argued from the perspective of the UK (both before and after the Brexit referendum): To downplay or overlook the advantages and further economic potential of this enormous alliance is to make a huge error. It is my strongly-held belief that there is also a major opportunity in the Commonwealth for India to lead a trade and investment agenda that could launch it into a more central role on the international stage. For all its member countries, the Commonwealth is an organisation of the future, not just the past.

From an Indian perspective, a proactive Commonwealth trade and investment agenda could carry with it key benefits. Firstly, as key parts of the world are beginning to turn inward, India and the UK could take a leading role in opening up the free trading opportunities around the world that continue to be key drivers of global prosperity. Secondly, as India looks to develop its penetration into vital emerging African markets, the Commonwealth could help India to realise its ambitious USD 90 billion African trade target. Finally, as India continues its ascent in international affairs as a potential superpower, the Commonwealth could be a very valuable conduit for spreading its values of democracy, tolerance and empowerment. These are values that Indian business can take around the world as part of this hugely geographically diverse organisation, and that also positively distinguish the Indian brand from some of its rival competitors.

The last two decades have seen a transformation in the India–UK trade relationship as India has become a major foreign investor. With Indian companies employing well over 100,000 people in Britain and owning hugely well-known brands including Jaguar and Tetley's, India has become the third-largest investor in the UK after the US and France. This is clearly a partnership of equals, equals that could work together in the interests of the Commonwealth.

Key, however, is that it is not just multinational conglomerates like Tata that are investing in the UK. Of the 800 or so Indian-owned businesses in the UK, we are seeing increasingly strong representation from India's small and medium-sized enterprises. Particularly in the areas of technology and telecoms, and pharmaceuticals and chemicals, Indian companies are showing that they can make it in the UK whether they have turnovers of £5 million or £250 million and beyond. But as well as being a demonstration of the positive India–UK relationship, this is also a case study for the Commonwealth. Owing to legal and language similarities, Indian companies can understand Britain and how to do business within it.

But despite this proven ability to thrive in the right foreign markets, the outlook for Indian exports has recently looked gloomy. In the last two years exports have contracted by almost 17 per cent—from USD 314.405 billion in fiscal 2013-14 to USD 261.136 billion in 2015-16. Export growth from India's micro, small and medium-size enterprises (MSMEs) has declined from 29.8 per cent in 2010-11 to 5.7 per cent in 2014-15. USD 90 billion African trade target for 2015 materialised in an actual figure of USD 56.67 billion, down from the previous year's USD 71.5 billion. And, according to the Confederation of Indian Industry, there are few signs of any immediate turnaround going into 2017.

If the Government of India is to hit its goal of doubling the country's exports to USD 900 billion and elevating its share of world trade from the current 2 per cent to 3.5 per cent by 2020 (as announced in India's Five Year Foreign Trade Policy of 2015), it may be that more imaginative approaches to foreign trade than are currently being deployed will be necessary. Of course, India has been sensible in recent years to engage heavily with its partners in the BRICS grouping and other international organisations with a more overt economic focus like the G20, but my case here is that there is another huge opportunity that is not being fully utilised.

The Commonwealth is a market of 2.2 billion citizens, 60 per cent of whom are under the age of thirty. By 2020 this will account for 40 per cent of the global workforce. The Commonwealth is adding to its middle class faster than any grouping so that, also by 2020, it is expected to contain 1 billion middle class consumers. Between 2013 and 2015, Commonwealth countries were expected to grow at a combined rate of 4.1 per cent in comparison to 1.8 per cent in the EU and 2.6 per cent in the US. Spanning some of the world's largest, smallest, richest and poorest countries, the Commonwealth has an enormously diverse set of markets with a combined GDP of USD 9.6 trillion in 2013. In addition to all this, owing to the shared use of the English language as well as shared values and similar legal and regulatory systems, the Commonwealth Secretariat estimates that trade costs between Commonwealth member countries are on an average 19 per cent lower than with non-Commonwealth countries.

During 2003-2013, trade in goods and services between Commonwealth countries expanded from USD 266 billion to USD 592 billion, registering an average annual growth rate of about 10 per cent. It is estimated that the intra-Commonwealth trade in goods and services in 2015 was USD 687 billion and is projected to surpass USD 1 trillion by 2020. In 2013, Commonwealth members' combined total exports of goods and services to all countries stood at USD 3.4 trillion, estimated to be 15 per cent of global exports.

These are notable figures, but they become particularly impressive when we consider that this growth and the Commonwealth's cheaper business costs have been achieved in the absence of any formal Commonwealth trade policy mechanisms. It has also been achieved against the fact that most Commonwealth members are active in their own formal regional trading arrangements.

This growth has been partly driven by, and has helped to further drive, India's own dramatic economic growth over the same period. Indian trade with the Commonwealth increased markedly between 2004 and 2014 with total Indian Commonwealth exports now worth nearly USD 100 billion. India's share of intra-Commonwealth services exports now accounts for 12 per cent of the USD 140 billion whilst India has a 16 per cent share in the USD 525 billion total of intra-Commonwealth goods exports. Commonwealth countries are amongst India's most significant trading partners. Five Commonwealth countries—Bangladesh, Malaysia, Singapore, Sri Lanka and the UK—feature amongst the top fifteen importers of Indian goods and services, whilst Australia, Nigeria, South Africa and Kenya are amongst India's fastest growing trade partners.

Therefore, as well as looking towards its formal trading blocs and bilateral relationships, India should also be looking much harder at the opportunities of the Commonwealth to achieve the trading growth that it desires. It has been projected that relatively modest coordinated trade facilitation measures and improvements in logistics would increase Commonwealth exports by £86 billion annually, boosting Commonwealth GDP by £122 billion and creating 24 million new jobs. But what the network currently lacks is the leadership that could put such an agenda into practice. If India were to take up a full and central role in the Commonwealth, working in partnership with the UK and other key member countries, it could provide the solution to this vacuum. The upcoming Commonwealth Trade Ministers Meeting in London in 2017 and the Commonwealth Business Forum and Heads of Government Meeting also in the UK in 2018 could be ideal places to start.

Deepening economic ties with Africa has become a key Indian strategic goal. With its abundant natural resources, status as the continent with the fastest economic growth in the world and rapidly-increasing population, it is easy to see why. India's progress here has certainly been impressive. The third India–Africa Forum Summit, held in Delhi in 2015, brought together representatives from all fifty-four African countries with forty-one represented at heads of state/government level. India unveiled plans to inject USD 10 billion worth of finance into a host of African development projects whilst pledging grant assistance of USD 600 million. But competition remains strong. In 2015, China promised USD 60 billion in assistance and loans to boost African development whilst Chinese trade with Africa, at around USD 200 billion, dwarfs India's USD 90 billion target.

Nurturing trade with the Commonwealth could help India get closer to this figure and would help it become a more effective counterbalance in the region. The Commonwealth contains eighteen African nations including by far the largest two economies in South Africa and Nigeria. Whilst this makes it a superb initial platform for greater African integration, a coherent African trade and development agenda with the entire Commonwealth network behind it would be one that would bring together a joint economic capacity on par with any in the world. Equally, in the Indian Ocean Rim, where China is also looking to vigorously press its own trading agenda, a more united Commonwealth with India at its forefront could again act as a counterbalance. Finally, with the BRICS grouping increasingly led by China and the South Asian Association for Regional Cooperation struggling with its own internal tensions—an Indian led Commonwealth with a clear trade and investment agenda is India's chance to drive its own international network and accelerate its rise as a central global player.

Better utilising the Commonwealth as a network for trade and investment also benefits India in terms of expanding the projection of its soft power. As part of its founding principles, the Commonwealth already has in place commitments to the promotion of democracy, peace and security, good governance, sustainable development and gender equality to name just a few. Developing a business agenda through this framework would signal to countries within and outside of the network that it means to act as a force for good in the international system with a sustainable economic growth model at its roots. This is an agenda that the Commonwealth Enterprise and Investment Council is also already pushing. With its mandate for promoting investment and employment opportunities in member states, as well as helping to establish the 'conditions for growth' across the network, the foundations for more coordinated activity amongst governments is already in place.

In conclusion, there is a significant business case for India developing a full and central role for itself within the Commonwealth. This underutilised network has already generated a hugely-impressive record for economic growth in the absence of any formal government policy mechanisms to bring this about. Now, at a time of stagnating global trade and uncertainty, it is clearly an opportune moment for member states to coordinate in a more active fashion. India, with its status as one of the most populous and fastest-growing countries in the world is in a prime position to lead such an agenda. With huge opportunities available across the Commonwealth, India can use the Commonwealth network to launch a dynamic new international trade and investment agenda and, in doing so, signal to its partners that it has well and truly arrived upon the international stage.

Lord Marland is Chair of the Commonwealth Enterprise and Investment Council (CWEIC).

The Imperatives of an Enhanced Security Connect

Lt General Syed Ata Hasnain

As a second-generation Indian military professional (father also being from the British Indian Army), belonging to a regiment which proudly wears its scarlet lanyard on the right shoulder due to its erstwhile royal status, student of Indian history and someone educated in a Church of England school replete with a British principal and headmaster, I surely can claim I had the right credentials as an Indian to attend the Royal College of Defence Studies (RCDS) programme in 2006. It was a year-long exchange at the famous Seaford House located at Belgravia, a stone's throw from the Buckingham Palace. One realises just how comfortable an Indian feels in London or anywhere in the UK; it is just that the environment is so 'Indian'. A military professional feels even more comfortable as the organisation of the UK's armed forces, the Ministry of Defence and even the concept and system of training are very familiar. The strong legacy of the British Indian armed forces and its retention in good measure by the Indian armed forces, especially the Indian Army, makes for greater endearment; the Regimental system, for instance, being a colonial legacy, yet found to be the best practice in terms of organisational effectiveness. Thus once Brigadier (later Maj Gen) Graham Binns, my sponsor in the UK army, member of the course, had ascertained that I could 'actually speak and understand the English language', I was on my own to ascertain what the UK was all about, with special reference to its relationship with India, its strategic and security compulsions and just how the two countries could mesh together the responses to future challenges.

Travelling the UK extensively, visiting a large number of military institutions and bases and getting exposure to the way the UK does business of governance and security give a clear impression that it lives by the byline— 'stability, security and prosperity'. That is what a like-minded nation such as India also believes in: The prosperity of its people through promotion of partnerships and cooperation which give rise to stability and security.

The relationship between the UK and India is a historic one. The Indian political, administrative and judicial system is largely UK-driven in that the practices adopted by the colonial rulers hardly needed much change till much later after Independence. The Indian Constitution is inspired by many constitutions but mainly by the British. Most importantly, the customs and many traditions the British left behind in India continue to be followed purely on their merit. The relationship between the two countries has always remained warm and friendly but the Cold War period prevented this from cementing into anything strategic. Post-1989, India has been through a period of major challenges in modernising and securing itself in the light of new threats. Equally, the UK has been one of the major partners of the US through the Cold War but was left with a degree of tentativeness and uncertainty in handling its future strategic and security needs after 1989. After approximately thirty years of this evolving uncertainty, both the UK and India are at a crucial juncture with broad understanding of the challenges before the world and the two nations in particular, many being common. The tentativeness of the last thirty years prevented a full-blooded relationship based on shared values and perceptions. Perhaps the take-off stage has arrived now. Brexit must be considered for the opportunity rather than for the procedural hurdles which come in the way of implementation of processes until the UK is clear off European controls.

THREATS AND OPPORTUNITIES

Prime Minister Modi's visit to the UK in November 2015 and the visit of Prime Minister Theresa May to India in November 2016 have opened new opportunities and reaffirmed ongoing cooperation in economics, tackling climate change, countering terror and organised crime and most specifically in the field of defence and security.

Violent Extremism and Ideological Radicalism

In allotting priority within the spectrum of threats, the problem of violent extremism and radical ideology probably stand out. The UK and India are both nations which respect multiculturalism and plurality. This is based on mutual respect between different faiths and ethnicities and the freedom to follow one's practices without impinging on the beliefs of others. Such systems which provide freedom and liberty are sometimes exploited by those with radical belief. While both the UK and India have much respect for those who follow the great faith of Islam, the two nations cannot permit radical groups from within Islam to attempt spreading their ideology which promotes intolerance and violence. The UK has been the target of radical groups who have attempted influencing the immigrant population exploiting the freedom and liberties that the UK guarantees. Similarly, India has been in the cross wires of radical extremists and sponsors of terror for over thirty years who have been trying to instigate the minority population of Muslims whose outlook is essentially Indian. At present, it is yet low on the list of target nations of the West Asia-based groups. However, it is a matter of time that this threat too may manifest and add to the threat from Pakistan and other parts of South Asia.

Both the UK and India are experienced in handling intelligence, follow-up, terminal-end terrorist actions and have best practices for the same. However, both need to add their conjoint weight to the early finalisation of the Comprehensive Convention on International Terrorism and isolate those nations which place impediments in the way of identifying and naming nations and groups involved in employing terror for their strategic goals. If they decide to do so, there is enough common ground to strategise on this.

Finance forms the bedrock of capability of terror organisations, especially in an increasingly-networked world. Both nations have cyber technologies developed to cater to this threat but need cooperation to establish obstacles and firewall the free flow of such funds. Exchange of technology and experience will benefit both immensely.

It is well recognised that the world is late in propounding counter-radicalisation and de-radicalisation programmes backed by the understanding of nuances of ideology which drive the spread of extremist philosophies. It is well known and established that Islam is a faith of peace hijacked by unscrupulous elements through spread of spurious ideas slickly packaged and delivered mainly with the help of social media. The UK has many strategic think tanks and academic research of a high order. Similarly, India has a large Muslim population largely moderate in belief. It also has schools of Islamic thinking, jurisprudence and interpretation. The strategic think tank culture has also arrived in India in large measure. The merger of research and joint models of counter and de-radicalisation can form one of the cornerstones of cooperation in the strategic sphere to safeguard both nations. This will need a drive well beyond that by the strategic community alone and will need to involve political leaderships and clergy too.

NUCLEAR POWER COOPERATION

The Civil Nuclear Cooperation Agreement signed between the two countries in November 2015 provides the opportunity to facilitate working together towards cleaner energy and benefit controls over climate change. It will also benefit third country partners by assisting them in addressing their development challenges in a wholly demand-driven manner. India's entry into all export control regimes is strongly supported by the UK and this must be leveraged for better effect.

TRANSNATIONAL AND CYBERCRIME

Organised transnational crime is a serious threat to both nations. It is through information sharing, operational cooperation and exchange of best practices to disrupt and dismantle criminal networks and bringing the perpetrators to justice, that this menace can be curbed. Fugitives from India are known to exploit the UK's extradition law, which needs to be prevented more seriously. This will be a true demonstration of intent. In the cyber-field the freedom of the internet is guaranteed by both nations. The proposed Cyber Security Training Centre of Excellence needs to be taken forward in an early time frame to allow the proliferation of expertise, training and capability.

GEOPOLITICAL AND GEOSTRATEGIC AREAS OF CONCERN

In a world changing rapidly, consultation is a dire need. The establishment of an annual senior official South Asia dialogue covering security, including terrorism, connectivity and maritime issues agreed during the visit of PM Modi in November 2015 will provide the means of such consultation and needs to be energised. India's geostrategic location assists the UK to maintain a 'midway contact' to its interests in the Far East and the Indo-Pacific region. The evident trust between the two nations needs to be converted to action. Much of this can be achieved if there is 'strategic convergence' in thinking between the intelligence and defence communities of both nations. At present it appears that we like to imagine and believe that there is convergence and trust purely because of the past warmth. However, that warmth was relevant to those times and never really converted into anything strategic despite the fact that the ideals of democracy as followed by the UK were and are best followed in India.

Leading the geostrategic considerations is Afghanistan although that may be classified as the core centre of the area of concern. It is the region around Afghanistan extending into Central Asia and Pakistan and increasingly into the western Indian Ocean which needs the attention of both nations. In the late nineteenth and early twentieth centuries the British Empire handled this entire geographical expanse as part of the Great Game. The Great Game was a series of political, diplomatic and military measures to secure spheres of influence to keep away the southward encroachment by the Russian empire. The same area is today in the throes of the New Great Game of which India is compulsorily an important part. However, it is all about access to the heart of Asia and reverse access to the ocean to facilitate flow of energy, trade and other forms of economics through the Belt and Road Initiative of China. India's denial of access to Central Asia, led and sponsored by Pakistan, forces it to look at other avenues to Afghanistan and Central Asia, chief being the Iranian port of Chabahar. The New Great Game also has a recent addition to it—the advent of radical ideology with the potential relocation of ISIS (Daesh) once forced out of Iraq and Syria. The complexity of such a game is understood by very few nations. The UK perhaps understands it the best having majorly led the Great Game. Thus the expanding influence of China, the rising potential of Russia–Pakistan cooperation, the uncertainty about Afghanistan and the frailty of the Iran Nuclear Deal in its implementation, are all going to adversely affect India–UK interests in different ways. Given the UK's long experience in handling such complex regions, albeit under different circumstances, both India and the UK can be in regular strategic consultation. The UK also has the experience of its physical presence in Afghanistan where India has deep interests too in the management of the complexities. India has leveraged its soft power there. The varied experience of both nations can only be to mutual advantage.

In the geopolitical and geostrategic spheres, the other area of mutual interest is the Indo-Pacific region where China's brazen attitude in the South China Sea forms a part of its global ambitions of domination. The UK has a history of handling Southeast Asia till as late as the seventies. Its interests as part of Western alliances continue to run in the area to ensure the freedom of navigation for much of the world's trade. India too is now involved more intimately with its Act East policy. This is again an area for consultation and action together as part of a larger group of nations who have deep interests in preventing hegemonic domination of other bigger powers.

A linkage between the UK and India left wide open and yet unexploited is the Commonwealth. The outreach to Africa by both nations can be through this medium as it was some years ago. It is also an appropriate club to garner greater support for India's candidature for the permanent membership of the UN Security Council, a proposal which the UK wholeheartedly supports.

DEFENCE COLLABORATION

Defence collaboration is a vast area for cooperation between nations with close bonds, trust and common perceptions of threats. The spectrum includes doctrine, training and transfer of strategic capability between the two nations, including defence technologies and manufacturing in areas of mutual interest. This was one of the major areas which came up for discussion during Prime Minister Modi's visit to the UK. There is a world of opportunity to be exploited and it is not important to identify each such facet of technology or sphere of cooperation in this essay. More important perhaps is to briefly identify why this did not happen in the past. Were there institutional hurdles or simply a lack of convergence of perception and a will to get things done?

As earlier emphasised, India happened to be in the Soviet camp during the heydays of the Cold War. Soviet antipathy to everything British goes back many decades and India was one of the bones of contention for this as the prime objective of the Great Game of the late nineteenth and early twentieth centuries. Post-Independence, India's close strategic partnership with the Soviet Union, although a major advantage during the Indo-Pak conflict of 1971, became the reason for lack of trust with the UK. Peripherally there was no Indo-UK discord or standoff but what could have been a natural strategic courtship never emerged. After 1989 too, India's emergence from the socialist era was slow and perhaps not very reassuring to the entire West, not the UK alone. In spite of clear threats on its borders and the Jammu & Kashmir asymmetric war sponsored by Pakistan, India did not accord the required priority to upgradation of its military capability. Procedures remained archaic and the rules of business antiquated.

India's chief weakness lies in its inability to undo the mammoth public sector undertakings which has been the cause of the low quality products the Indian armed forces have contended with all these years. With 70 per cent of the capital requirements being imported and procedures for the same so bureaucratic, it took years to fructify deals into delivery. There is a sincere effort to decontrol acquisitions through new procedures. A wholly new Defence Procurement Procedure had been put together under former Defence Minister Manohar Parrikar. The changes in FDI rules may not have yet attracted the kind of potential which was expected. This is primarily because the decontrol mechanism is a work in progress and a need to convince potential partners remains. With a country such as the UK with one of our oldest embassies/high commissions, there is no reason why a defence industry segment cannot supplement the offices of the defence attaché.

India's security requirements are manifold but chief among them is the capability gap with China. Even some of Pakistan's ground-based systems are qualitatively superior—night-fighting capability for instance. It needs transfer of technology by advanced countries who are reluctant to part with high-end technology for reasons of their own security. With India's multilateral approach as against alliance-based approach, the challenge of security glitches related to imported technology should be something of the past.

Conclusion

Special relationships are based on historical connections and trust. It is unfortunate that the intervening forty-five years of the Cold War found India and the UK on opposite sides. Despite that, the relationship remained warm without converting into anything strategic. The connect between the Indian armed forces and the erstwhile British armed forces based upon two centuries of association, albeit under colonial rule, remained one of the cornerstones of the relationship. It is only natural that they should remain central to the idea of an enhanced strategic connect between the two nations. There is history to be exploited and yet a future waiting with opportunities, and both nations appear to have the will to take this to a natural culmination of aspirations.

Lt Gen Syed Ata Hasnain is a highly decorated officer of the Indian Army and the former Commander of the Kashmir Corps.

India and the UK: Post-Brexit Security and Defence Cooperation

Rahul Roy-Chaudhury

India and the UK have a strong shared history, speak the same language and share a commitment to democratic values. They are described as having a 'natural partnership'[1] and their formal 'comprehensive strategic partnership' was upgraded in 2010 to an 'enhanced partnership'. Their elites are comfortable and familiar with each other.

But the bilateral relationship has not reached the dizzying heights of their mutual rhetoric. Several impediments continue to be in place. Yet, with the UK government emphasising trade relations with India as a top priority[2] and India seeking additional political and diplomatic leverages to become a 'leading power' in the international system[3], a unique post-Brexit opportunity exists for boosting India–UK security and defence cooperation and collaboration.

'Natural Partnership'?

For India, the UK is important, as the fifth-largest economy in the world; the largest G20 investor in India, whose capital is the leading global financial centre; a permanent member of the influential UN Security Council and a country which wields considerable South Asian and global influence through its enviable comprehensive network of strategic partnerships.[4] The UK was the first permanent member of the UN Security Council to call for India's permanent membership of a reformed UN Security Council, having supported India's bid for membership since 2002. It has welcomed India's joining of the Missile Technology Control Regime (MTCR) as strengthening global non-proliferation objectives. And, the UK is a strong supporter of early Indian membership of the Nuclear Suppliers Group (NSG), a top foreign policy objective of Indian Prime Minister Narendra Modi.

For the UK, India is important as, a fast-growing and seventh-largest economy in the world; the third-largest foreign investor in the UK with more investments in the UK than the rest of the EU; the second-largest employer in the UK employing roughly 110,000 people with approximately 800 Indian-owned companies operating in the UK; a key country for future global climate change impact and a country with a rising foreign policy profile seeking increased roles and responsibilities on the world stage.

But over the past few years, the India–UK power dynamics has changed, with India becoming more important to the UK than the UK to India.[5] This is expected to intensify with India's economy projected to grow and overtake the UK as the fifth-largest global economy in 2018 (in the same year as India's defence spending is projected to overtake the UK's defence spending), as well as the impact of Brexit, with the UK emphasising trade relations with India as a top priority. Yet, those in India who feel that the UK today is simply a relative 'declining' power in strategic terms with little relevance to the aspirations of a 'rising' India, are short-sighted.

Nonetheless, there are several impediments and irritants to India–UK bilateral relations that have prevented the emergence of a true strategic partnership.

First, Indian sensitivity over British colonial history. Even as India celebrates its seventieth year of independence from Britain, aspects of this relationship can, at times, be extremely 'prickly' with Indian officials in the centre-right Indian government and public sentiments sensitive over insults or slights, perceived or real. This can also be seen in terms of the controversy over an apology from the UK for the Jallianwala Bagh massacre in 1919, India's demand for the return of the Kohinoor diamond, and the call for the

UK to make repatriation payments for its colonial rule, all of which result in a certain 'sharpness' in India's diplomatic relations unique to Britain.

Second, Indian suspicion over the UK's perceived bias towards Pakistan. In the past, India was annoyed with the UK's 'hyphenation' of India with Pakistan. While this 'hyphenation' is now more or less over, New Delhi still remains suspicious over the UK's perceived bias towards Pakistan. The Indian security establishment believes the UK could do far more than it is currently doing to curb cross-border terrorism emanating from Pakistan. The UK government, on the other hand, feels that such a view is grossly simplified and its influence over the Pakistan army and the Inter-Services Intelligence (ISI) is exaggerated. It also points to ongoing India–UK cooperation on counterterrorism which has effectively helped prevent terror attacks on India, while at the same time seeking to bring the Pakistani perpetrators of the 2008 Mumbai and the 2016 Uri terror attacks to justice. At the same time, the UK is concerned over any sudden deterioration in regional stability, and encourages India and Pakistan to resume their official-level bilateral dialogue.

Third, Indian concerns over the Kashmir dispute, Sikh extremism and caste issues in the UK. The Indian government believes the UK government 'allows' the Houses of Parliament to occasionally debate the Kashmir dispute between India and Pakistan. Moreover, the British government's protestation that the UK is a democracy and cannot stifle debate is not perceived as convincing and reflects poorly in Delhi. On 19 January 2017, for example, Members of Parliament debated and approved a motion on Kashmir that noted '...breaches of international human rights on the Indian side of the Line of Control in Kashmir' and called on the British government to '... encourage Pakistan and India to...establish a long-term solution on the future governance of Kashmir based on the right of the Kashmiri people to determine their own future in accordance with the provisions of UN Security Council resolutions'.[6] With the Indian government strongly opposed to any external 'third party' intervention on the Kashmir dispute or the idea of a plebiscite in Kashmir, the official British response by the Minister for Asia, Alok Sharma, clarified that 'the long-standing position of the UK is that it can neither prescribe a solution to the situation in Kashmir nor act as a mediator. It is for the Governments of India and Pakistan to find a lasting resolution, taking into account the wishes of the Kashmiri people'.[7] Yet, the latter part of Sharma's formulation is itself perceived as an irritant by the Indian government, which feels that Kashmiris regularly exercise their right to vote in Indian state and general elections. Moreover, regular British Foreign Office ministerial references to 'Indian-administered Kashmir' as opposed to 'Jammu & Kashmir' are also seen as irritants.[8]

India is also concerned over the UK's perceived leniency in keeping a tight leash on Sikh separatist activities in the UK, marked by the March 2016 lifting of the ban on the International Sikh Youth Federation (ISYF), which had been proscribed as a terrorist organisation in 2001 by the British government for attacks against Indian officials. The Cameron government had justified this on the basis that there was 'now not sufficient evidence to support a reasonable belief that the ISYF is currently concerned in terrorism as defined by Section 3(5) of the Terrorism Act 2000'.[9]

In 2013, a provision against caste discrimination was inserted into the Equality Act 2010 on the assumption that the caste system existed in the UK's Indian diaspora. Although the previous coalition government of Prime Minister David Cameron had indicated that legislation to this effect would be introduced in Parliament during the summer of 2015, this was reviewed, and in September 2016 the UK government announced it would first conduct a public consultation on the issue. Nonetheless, Indian analysts are concerned that such possible legislation could give rise to sectarian tensions among the Hindu community in the UK.

Fourth, there is an influential perception in India that the UK is very slow, and at times, unhelpful, in cases of deportation/extradition but expects full cooperation from the Indian side in cases of interest to it. Yet, a new round of the bilateral dialogue on matters related to extradition and mutual legal assistance was held in late February 2017, with progress towards the extradition from the UK of Indian liquor baron Vijay Mallya on a bank loan default case.

Fifth, competition to the UK from other major and regional powers. At the start of India's economic rise a decade-and-a-half ago, the UK was one of India's top five strategic partners, with the others variously being the US, Russia, France and Israel. But with India's high economic growth and consequent strategic outreach, new and prospective strategic partners have fast emerged to court India, including Japan, Australia, Germany, Vietnam, and more recently, the UAE. For India today, the UK is no longer one of its top five strategic partners.

As a result, bilateral prime ministerial visits have remained limited. Despite the UK being the first country after Russia with which India agreed to an annual exchange of Heads of Government visits in September 2004, only six British prime ministerial visits to India have taken place since then–Tony Blair in September 2005, Gordon Brown in January 2008, David Cameron in July 2010, February 2013 and November 2013 (en route to the Commonwealth Summit in Sri Lanka), and new Prime Minister Theresa May in November 2016. Both Cameron's and May's first visit to India took place within weeks of their becoming prime minister; India was also the destination of May's first major bilateral visit outside the EU as prime minister. In contrast, only two bilateral Indian prime ministerial visits to the UK have taken place since September 2004, with Dr Manmohan Singh's visit in October 2006 and Narendra Modi's visit in November 2015 (Singh's March-April 2009 visit was for the G20 summit).

Brexit's Impact

In the short-term, Brexit has already disrupted the momentum in India–UK relations that was to have taken place following Modi's visit to the UK in November 2015. This visit—the first Indian prime ministerial bilateral visit to the UK in nearly a decade—had set in place several ambitious and challenging objectives for a transformation of the bilateral relationship.

Two features stood out from this visit.[10] British Prime Minister David Cameron spent two full days with Modi, signalling his personal commitment to boosting the bilateral relationship. Both premiers also spoke of the tremendous potential of the bilateral relationship for mutual prosperity and international security, implicitly acknowledging that it needed to be transformed. Significant economic and investment decisions took place, alongside the opportunity for Modi to address some 60,000 British Indians and Non-Resident Indians (NRI) at Wembley Stadium.

But now, amidst the reality of a 'hard Brexit', the timeline of this ambitious objective of transforming India–UK relations will realistically need to be revised and reset. For the next two years and more, the UK government is expected to be largely consumed politically with defining its relations with the EU (to be followed by the next British general elections in 2020), notwithstanding its rhetoric of a 'global Britain' and of an 'outward-looking nation'.

The UK government has emphasised that trade relations with India and the finalisation of a new India–UK free trade deal will be its top priority.[11] But this will have to await the UK's finalisation of its relations with the EU, not expected before the summer of 2019. Yet, in the interim, there remains considerable potential and scope for boosting cooperation and collaboration in bilateral security and defence, areas which crucially remain largely immune to the quirks of Brexit.

SECURITY COOPERATION—THE KEY

COUNTERTERRORISM

Counterterrorism cooperation has emerged as the Modi government's principle security objective and top priority for international security cooperation. India and the UK have cooperated on counterterrorism since January 2002, with the formation of the joint working group (JWG) on terrorism.[12] Yet, the Indian security establishment feels the UK is not as forthcoming as India's other 'strategic partners' in condemning cross-border terrorism, perhaps, owing to Pakistani sensitivities.

Yet, significantly, key progress in counterterrorism was made during Modi's visit to the UK in November 2015. The India–UK joint statement for the first time named Pakistan-based militant group, the Lashkar-e-Taiba (LeT), responsible for the November 2008 Mumbai terror attacks, and the Haqqani network, behind the July 2008 attacks on the Indian embassy in Kabul, and sought to disrupt their financial and tactical support. Both sides also called for Pakistan to bring the perpetrators of the 2008 Mumbai terror attack to justice. May also strongly condemned the September 2016 terrorist attack on the Indian army brigade headquarters in Uri in Jammu & Kashmir, and also called for Pakistan to bring the perpetrators of the 2016 Pathankot attack to justice. The Modi–May joint statement went further by calling for 'strong measures against all those who encourage, support and finance terrorism, provide sanctuary to terrorists and terror groups, and falsely extol their virtues. There should be no glorification of terrorists or efforts to make a distinction between good and bad terrorists'.[13] But, the UK did not agree to go as far as India would have wished to formally include the term 'cross-border terrorism' in the joint statement.

CYBERSECURITY

For India, the UK is a favoured partner for cybersecurity cooperation and collaboration. Following India's participation in the London Conference on Cyberspace in 2011, the two governments held their first structured dialogue on cooperation on cyber issues in October 2012, and agreed to work on areas of common interest in the cyber domain. Since then, India has developed a formal cybersecurity framework and in March 2015 appointed a cybersecurity chief, whilst evolving its policy on international cyber-governance issues to seek greater cooperation with the West. During Modi's visit to the UK, both sides agreed to establish a Cyber Security Training Centre of Excellence to train a million India cybersecurity professionals, and the UK offered assistance to set up a new Indian cybercrime coordination centre.

CIVIL NUCLEAR COOPERATION

In November 2015, India and the UK signed a much-delayed bilateral civil nuclear agreement. This includes exchange of best practices, especially in areas like decommissioning, where Britain has superior technologies. Britain's advantage in this area in relation to other nuclear powers is the potential it offers to India for industrial cooperation as well as collaboration on research and development.[14]

DEFENCE MANUFACTURING AND PROCUREMENT

India's aim to modernise and expand its armed forces has led to it becoming one of the world's top five global defence importers and spenders in 2016. It is projected that India's defence spending will surpass the UK's in 2018, rising from £25 billion in 2010 to £51 billion in 2020, against expectations of £43 billion for the UK in 2020.[15] India is also seeking to develop its own defence manufacturing industry. The UK's largest defence company BAE Systems— the third largest in the world by revenue—has been 'making in India' for the past fifty-plus years, in partnership with India's Hindustan Aeronautical Limited (HAL). This includes the licensed-production/assembly of the Jaguar combat aircraft in the 1970s, the Sea Harriers in the 1980s and since 2008, the Hawk Advanced Jet Trainer (AJT), of which 99 of 123 have been 'built' in India. In July 2014, MBDA UK signed a contract to equip the Indian Air Force's (IAF) Sepecat/Hindustan Aeronautics Jaguar strike aircraft with Advanced Short-Range Air-to-Air Missiles (ASRAAM)[16]. In November 2016, the Indian government agreed to a deal with the US to acquire 145 BAE Systems M777 lightweight artillery guns. But British defence companies are keen to further enhance the ease of doing defence business in India.

Afghanistan, the Gulf and Maritime Security

Both India and the UK have suffered as a result of the unstable security environment in Afghanistan and the 'safe havens' and sustenance provided by Pakistan to the Afghan Taliban and the Haqqani network. As a result, they have a shared interest in ensuring the future stability and security of Afghanistan.[17] Both governments agree that 'a political settlement in Afghanistan has to be Afghan-owned and Afghan-led and will succeed only if the Taliban insurgency abandons violence and abides by democratic norms'.[18] But, perhaps, like the US, the UK could formally recognise India's contribution to stability in Afghanistan, especially after New Delhi was stung by the perceived the UK support towards an MoU between the ISI and the Afghan intelligence agency NDS (National Directorate of Security) in May 2015.

The Gulf region is an intrinsic part of the Indian Ocean, which the Modi government views as its 'near and extended neighbourhood'. Over 7 million Indian nationals are resident in the Gulf, with growing Indian dependence on energy and investments from the region. Even as India builds its defence and security ties in the Gulf, the UK retains its long-standing comprehensive network of strategic partnerships in the region.

Conclusion

Significantly, in the past two years a multidimensional dialogue architecture for security cooperation between India and the UK has been put in place. In November 2015, the new Defence and International Security Partnership (DISP) was set up with particular emphasis on strengthening cybersecurity, counterterrorism and maritime security. In addition to regular prime ministerial summits, new national security advisor (NSA)-level talks were to take place along with defence ministers and service chiefs meetings, as well as regular senior official meetings.[19]

On counterterrorism, the key security objective of the Modi government, bilateral cooperation could be thickened and deepened. In February 2017, Prime Minister Modi told a group of eight visiting Members of Parliament from the UK that India and the UK were 'natural partners in the global fight against terrorism'.[20] Following China's veto of India's proposal to designate Jaish-e-Mohammed (JeM) chief Masood Azhar as a 'global terrorist' by the UN in December 2016, the UK co-sponsored, along with the US and France, a similar resolution tabled at the UN on 19 January 2017 to freeze access to his financial accounts and ban foreign travel. Unfortunately, like the previous resolution this one was also blocked by China.

Greater sharing of intelligence to prevent, deter and disrupt terror attacks on India and the UK should also take place. Surprisingly, the Modi–May November 2016 joint statement did not explicitly name any terrorist organisation, in contrast to the previous Modi–Cameron November 2015 joint statement. Terrorist groups such as the Pakistan-based JeM, responsible for the 2001 attack on the Indian Parliament and the January 2016 Pathankot attack, should be formally named in future joint statements, along with Dawood Ibrahim. There should be 'actionable' exchanges of intelligence related to money laundering, related crimes and terrorism financing. The UK could also seek the early adoption of the Comprehensive Convention on International Terrorism (CCIT), proposed by India in the UN two decades ago. With both countries seeking to prevent future terror attacks on their mainland, prospects for enhanced cooperation on intelligence-sharing and counterterrorism could become a key positive 'game changer' in the India–UK relationship.

India–UK cyber-relations, despite its success, also have the potential to expand through the finalisation of a framework for bilateral cybersecurity.

Opportunities for greater bilateral consultation on regional security issues exist in the Arabian Gulf region, the Indian Ocean and South Asia. In November 2015, both governments agreed to formalise their annual senior official dialogue on South Asia, including maritime security issues.[21] At his major mid-term foreign policy speech at New Delhi's Raisina Dialogue in January 2017, Modi explicitly mentioned the importance of maritime security and the Indian Ocean.[22] At the same conference, the UK Foreign Secretary Boris Johnson publicly acknowledged India's role as a 'vital force for stability' in the Indian Ocean Region,[23] with its own aspirations to sail the waters of the Indian Ocean with its two new aircraft carriers. This could provide a strategic opportunity for India to forge a consensus on its deepening concerns over Chinese naval activities and presence in the Indian Ocean, including by the bolstering and expansion of bilateral naval exercises to a trilateral dimension with another like-minded country. An India–UK 'task force' could also be formed to see how best to 'take forward' India's bid for membership of the NSG as well as permanent membership of a reformed UN Security Council.

Considerable potential also exists for furthering defence cooperation and collaboration. But the UK needs to overcome a perception by the Indian security establishment that British companies are interested in merely selling and not jointly manufacturing in India, hence, it is more of a transactional arrangement. Yet, 99 of the 123 Hawk aircraft have been assembled in India. The recent BAE Systems M777 deal provides the establishment of a final assembly, integration and testing facility for the artillery system in partnership with the Mahindra Group, a first by any foreign defence company in India. HAL and BAE Systems have equally funded and developed jointly the new dual-role combat-capable Advanced Hawk for Indian and export markets. This was formally unveiled at the Aero India air show in Bengaluru in February 2017.

Further defence cooperation also seems possible on aircraft-carrier technologies. At the same time, the UK needs to further operationalise and make public its commitment to make available to India cutting-edge military technology that it currently shares with its top international partners, in accordance with international obligations.

In this regard, British Foreign Secretary Boris Johnson in New Delhi in January 2017 stated that 'we have set up a joint working group to take things forward across the waterfront of issues—security, counterterrorism, intelligence-sharing…defence cooperation, technology-sharing. We want to do much, much more together and then of course, there is the whole free trade deal'.[24]

However, India–UK bilateral relations do not exist in a vacuum. While the UK may consider it is working sufficiently with India, other countries such as the US, Russia, France, Germany, Japan, Australia, Vietnam and the UAE are seeking to do even more with India. If the UK is to return as one of India's top five strategic partners, implementation of security and defence cooperation remains key, especially through key 'deliverables' or tangible dividends in the next year-and-a-half, during the period the UK is focused on defining its relations with the EU and before India begins to focus on its next general elections. This will also be fundamental in favourably positioning the India–UK relationship to quickly take advantage of the economic and trade dividends expected to take place after the next two or more years.

Rahul Roy-Chaudhury is the Senior Fellow for South Asia at the International Institute for Strategic Studies (IISS) in London.

ENDNOTES

1. Government of India, Ministry of External Affairs. 'India–UK Joint Statement during the visit of Prime Minister of the United Kingdom to India (India–UK Strategic Partnership looking forward to a renewed engagement: Vision for the decade ahead)', 7 November 2016, at http://mea.gov.in/bilateral-documents.htm?dtl/27584/indiauk+joint+statement+during+the+visit+of+prime+minister+of+the+united+kingdom+to+india+indiauk+strategic+partnership+looking+forward+to+a+renewed+engagement+vision+for+the+decade+ahead

2. UK Government. '£1 billion in deals from PM's trade mission to India', 10 November 2016 at https://www.gov.uk/government/news/1-billion-in-deals-from-pms-trade-mission-to-india

3. Mohan, C Raja. 'Making India a "Leading Power"', *Mint*, 6 April 2016, at http://www.livemint.com/Opinion/Xiw11wTk3zMHLbUw80ayWP/Making-India-a-leading-power.html

4. Roy-Chaudhury, Rahul. 'Why it's Short-Sighted to Think of the UK as a "Declining Power"', *The Wire*, 19 November 2015 at http://thewire.in/15918/why-its-short-sighted-to-think-of-the-uk-as-a-declining-power/

5. See Scott, David. 'The rise of India: UK perspectives,' in Miller, Manjari Chatterjee and Estrada, Kate Sullivan de (eds.). *India's rise at 70*, (International Affairs 93: 1 (2017)), p 165.

6. 'MPs debate Kashmir', at https://www.parliament.uk/business/committees/committees-a-z/commons-select/backbench-business-committee/news-parliament-2015/mps-debate-kashmir/

7. Ray, Ashis. 'Kashmir Debate in Britain,' *Asian Lite News*, 24 January 2017, at https://asianlite.com/news/asia-diaspora-news/ashis-ray-on-kashmir-debate-in-britain/

8. See, for example, 'Foreign Secretary condemns attack in Indian-administered Kashmir', 18 September 2016, at https://www.gov.uk/government/news/fco-press-release-foreign-secretary-condemns-attack-in-indian-administered-kashmir

9. Menon, Parvathi. 'UK lifts ban on Sikh separatist outfit', *The Hindu*, 19 March 2016, at http://www.thehindu.com/news/international/british-parliament-lifts-ban-on-sikh-terrorist-outfit/article8374978.ece.

10. Roy-Chaudhury, Rahul. op.cit., *The Wire*, 19 November 2015.

11. UK Government, 'Foreign Secretary's speech at Raisina Dialogue, New Delhi', 18 January 2017, at https://www.gov.uk/government/speeches/foreign-secretarys-speech-at-raisina-dialogue-new-delhi

12. Government of India, Ministry of External Affairs. 'The New Delhi Declaration: India And United Kingdom: Partnership For A Better And Safer World', 6 January 2002, at http://mea.gov.in/bilateral-documents.htm?dtl/7509/the+new+delhi+declaration+india+and+united+kingdom+partnership+for+a+better+and+safer+world

13. Government of India, op. cit., 7 November 2016.

14. Government of India, Department of Atomic Energy. 'Agreement between Government of India and Government of United Kingdom of Great Britain and Northern Ireland for co-operation in the peaceful uses of Nuclear Energy', 13 November 2015, at http://www.dae.nic.in/writereaddata/indo_uk_0116_new.pdf

15. Hollinger, Peggy. 'India moves into top five global defence spenders,' *Financial Times*, 12 December 2016, at https://www.ft.com/content/8404e57a-bfa1-11e6-9bca-2b93a6856354

16. Chandra, Atul. 'MBDA signs Indian ASRAAM contract,' *Flight Global*, 10 July 2014, at https://www.flightglobal.com/news/articles/mbda-signs-indian-asraam-contract-401260/

17. Roy-Chaudhury, Rahul. 'Shared Interests in "AfPak" Issues and Counter-Terrorism' in Johnson, Jo and Kumar, Rajiv (eds.). *Reconnecting Britain and India: Ideas for an Enhanced Partnership* (Academic Foundation, January 2012), p 67.

18. Government of India, Ministry of External Affairs, op.cit., 7 November 2016.

19. Roy-Chaudhury, Rahul. op.cit., *The Wire*, 19 November 2015.

20. 'India, UK are natural partners in global fight against terrorism: PM Modi', 14 February 2017, at https://article.wn.com/view/2017/02/14/India_UK_are_natural_partners_in_global_fight_against_terror_s/

21. UK Government, 'UK–India Defence and International Security Partnership', 12 November 2015, at https://www.gov.uk/government/news/uk-india-defence-and-international-security-partnership

22. Government of India, Ministry of External Affairs. 'Inaugural Address by Prime Minister Narendra Modi at Second Raisina Dialogue, New Delhi', 17 January 2017, at http://mea.gov.in/Speeches-Statements.htm?dtl/27948/Inaugural+Address+by+Prime+Minister+at+Second+Raisina+Dialogue+New+Delhi+January+17+2017

23. UK Government, 'Foreign Secretary's speech at Raisina Dialogue, New Delhi', op.cit., 18 January 2017.

24. Ministerial Address of Foreign Secretary Boris Johnson, Observer Research Foundation, "Raisina Dialogue 2017", 18 January 2017, New Delhi, *Minutes 31:58-32:41*. In the Q&A session, Boris Johnson responds, 19 January 2017, at https://www.youtube.com/watch?v=U6RcGf6hduE

Matching the UK's Strengths with India's Developmental Aspirations

Dr Gareth Price

The joint statement that resulted from Theresa May's visit to India in November 2016 set out a broad range of areas with the potential for greater interaction between the UK and India. The UK has been astute in recognising the benefit of engaging on areas in which India has a need, as opposed to pushing India on areas in which the UK has strengths but which may not match India's priorities. Yet while the agenda is broad and impressive, often the level of engagement on each individual issue could be deepened.

Moving forward, as the UK seeks to strengthen its relationship with India, is there a particular feature of global governance on which it could work with India to demonstrate the utility of the bilateral relationship? Alternatively, are there lessons from other countries which have sought to promote themselves within India?

For the first question, that of global governance, India frequently works on an issue-by-issue basis with like-minded countries. Thus, when promoting itself as a fast-growing economy, India has utilised the BRICS—Brazil, Russia, India, China and, later, South Africa. The BRICS grouping initially faced criticism from some Western commentators since the members do not share the same value system. This criticism missed the point in that the BRICS grouping is clearly not intended to promote shared values; its point was that it highlights an important source of global economic growth. In addition, the grouping faced criticism for not having an 'institution'. The response to this has been to create one: The BRICS Development Bank.

An alternative grouping which does share values as well as an aspiration for permanent membership of a reformed UN Security Council is the IBSA Dialogue Forum, comprising India, Brazil and South Africa. Formed in 2003, the IBSA grouping has frequently forged common positions when faced with particular regional or global challenges. For instance, IBSA led opposition to the position taken by the West in the 2003 World Trade Organisation (WTO) talks in Cancún, Mexico, and helped to forge a developing world bloc in the WTO.

Another pertinent grouping is the Indian Ocean Rim Association (IORA), which has a secretariat based in Mauritius and comprises twenty-one countries with a coastline on the Indian Ocean. India has long sought to strengthen IORA if not overtly to counter an increased Chinese presence in the Indian Ocean rather to enhance dialogue and engagement amongst littoral states.

So for the UK, is there a particular issue for which cooperation and engagement between the UK and India makes sense and for which a UK–India grouping could work together to come up with a shared approach or set of rules? While they may not be obvious partners, both countries have expressed a desire to work together on global governance issues. Many of the issues are already on the dialogue agenda for the UK and India. These include terrorism, radicalisation, cybersecurity and sustainable energy, for instance.

On each of these issues, there is scope for deeper and sustained dialogue that could, in time, come up with a set of rules or a shared approach to the issue under discussion. Were the UK to invest the time and resources and develop, with India, a common understanding of the issue and a common solution, this would send a powerful signal, as well as demonstrate—to India—that the UK is a useful global partner.

Many of the existing interactions are not as deep or sustained to actually facilitate the UK and India coming up with an agreed approach. There would be merit in choosing one issue—internet governance, for example—and investing additional resources to enable deeper mutual understanding.

For the second approach, are there lessons from other countries seeking to deepen their engagement with India? Of late, most Western countries have sought to promote themselves within India. India's importance to the West— both in relation to global challenges and as a place of economic opportunity— is a relatively recent development. While India's 1998 nuclear tests brought it sanctions, they also served to highlight its indigenous engineering base to some in Western countries. This human capacity started to become more integrated into global supply chains in the run-up to the year 2000, as fears of the Millennium Bug were widespread and India was identified as a country with human resources capable of tackling the threat. And it is from this point that Western countries started to wake up to India's potential.

Since then, India's economy has grown significantly. Less than twenty years ago, in 1998, India's nominal per capita income was just USD 425. Now it is almost five times higher, and much more in purchasing power parity terms.

Japan was one of the first 'Western' countries to spot India's potential, and through its technical and financial support, has facilitated the Delhi– Mumbai Industrial Corridor, a mega project—costing USD 90 billion and covering around 1,500 km between the two cities—to improve infrastructure and build up industrial zones. Japanese support for the construction of the Delhi Metro also served to popularise Japan amongst the metropolitan elite.

Next were the EU and the US. The latter delivered the US–India civil nuclear deal. While this may not have been quite the transformational deal initially imagined, the US's wooing of India is starting to pay dividends, through increased military-to-military cooperation.

The EU, unsurprisingly, has focused on trade. But the free trade agreement envisaged has not yet come to pass with blame shared between the two sides. Ironically, some of the more significant stumbling blocks to the EU–India FTA—in particular mobility of Indian professionals—are likely to be removed following the UK's decision to leave the EU. By channelling member states' expertise, more recently the EU has forged partnerships with India on water, clean energy and climate change. This pooling of expertise, partly in recognition of the reality of capacity constraints in India's bureaucracy, makes sense.

In each of these cases, the relationship has been developed predicated on India's needs, with the Western partner looking for issues in which they have deep-rooted expertise, which can be shared with India for mutual benefit. While the UK has shifted to trying to focus on India's policy priorities, problematically, post-referendum Britain appears more insular, despite rhetorically committing to a more internationalist perspective.

At the same time, the UK's flagship industries—in particular financial and legal services—are not priority areas for India. While there have been some positive developments for the former, with the introduction of masala bonds, it is difficult to make the case that the UK and Indian economies are complementary. German trade with India has risen significantly in recent years. This is because Germany manufactures the types of products wanted by emerging economies such as India. Meanwhile, the UK exports have flatlined as they do not provide the types of products that India wants. In similar vein, Chinese consumer preferences have shifted towards some luxury products produced by the UK. Indian consumers in general have not. In addition, India's primary ask of the UK is for greater visa access, a wish unlikely to be granted in contemporary Britain.

That said, is there an issue or sector which the UK could focus on in partnership with India's developmental aspirations? An area for which proven British expertise could be showcased and for which British commitment could run deep?

Education is the obvious area for enhanced collaboration. Higher education is a British strength, and numerous surveys suggest it is an Indian weakness. Many prominent Indians have been educated in the UK, and only five years ago almost 70,000 Indian students were enrolled in British universities. Now, however, that figure has fallen below 12,000, as the UK has sought to reduce inward migration. Many politicians believe that student numbers should be exempted from overall migration figures, but current restrictions on working in the UK postgraduation make other countries— notably Canada and Australia—more attractive options.

Hopefully, the current British mindset will change and Indian students will be seen as contributors to the economy. If not, the recent proposal of NITI Aayog—that foreign universities should be allowed to operate in India—offers some scope for optimism. While the process of opening Indian higher education up to foreign institutions—in whatever form—may be lengthy, British universities would be well advised to deepen collaborative research with Indian counterparts in the hope of opening campuses, whether alone or in partnership with existing Indian universities, at some stage in the future.

While India remains protectionist towards its financial and legal sectors, there has been some progress in British thinking. For several years, the UK approach was to blindly request that India open up its financial and legal sectors. More recently, the financial sector has asked itself how, given current constraints, it can make itself relevant to India's developmental needs. Infrastructure finance—with India's aspirational plans for Make in India, Digital India, Skill India and Smart Cities—is the obvious answer. London has established itself as the leading global centre for offshore rupee financing, issuing more than USD 1.1 billion of rupee-denominated bonds in recent months.

Beyond education, the question for the UK is whether to continue with a broad, if shallow, array of dialogues and collaborations or to focus on a smaller number and go deeper. A couple of years ago, the UK and India launched an official-level dialogue regarding Afghanistan. This was a positive initiative. If there is to be deeper collaboration on an issue, first both sides need to be clear that they are conceptualising the issue in a similar manner. In 2015, the Afghanistan dialogue was subsequently broadened and two separate dialogues were launched, one on South Asia and another on West Asia (the Middle East).

On a range of issues, both the conceptualisation of the problem and the national interests involved are currently markedly different. In terms of India's security concerns, terrorism emanating from Pakistan, and in India's view, facilitated by Pakistan's military, is a priority. The UK, however, values its relationship with Pakistan, enhanced by the Pakistani diaspora in the UK and underscored by the fact that most Pakistani political leaders have houses in London.

At times the UK has used its leverage for good, facilitating a meeting between the Afghan President Ashraf Ghani and Pakistani Prime Minister Nawaz Sharif, when relations between the two countries were strained. But more generally, there is a perception in Delhi that the UK is 'soft' on Pakistan. Given that infrequent windows of opportunity for dialogue between the two countries are generally slammed shut within weeks by terrorist attacks on India, there is a strong argument that current UK (and Western) policy towards Pakistan is failing in its stated objectives.

In the Middle East, the UK's interventionist approach sits ill at ease with India's more pragmatic non-interventionism. Interests too diverge. India's concerns include its reliance on petrochemicals from the Middle East, the security of its large diaspora spread across the region and the utility of the remittances that this diaspora provides. That said, India's role in the Middle East is increasing, highlighted by the fact that the guest of honour at India's 2017 Republic Day celebrations was the Crown Prince of Abu Dhabi. A sustained dialogue between the UK and India over developments in the Middle East can only serve to increase cognisance of divergent approaches and, through this dialogue, find areas for concrete collaboration.

Many of the subjects on which partnerships were announced during Theresa May's visit appear to be on the money—areas where experiences can be shared and best practices developed. For instance, understanding of the causes of radicalisation is an area rich with potential for collaboration. There are lessons to be learnt from India, which has proven remarkably resilient to Islamic radicalisation. As of the end of 2015, around 1,200 French citizens had travelled to join the Islamic State. India's Muslim population—of around 180 million—had contributed just twenty-five. However, complacency would be misplaced. As more and more Indians have access to smartphones, fears over the potential for online radicalisation are well grounded. Yet, as with many of the subjects picked for cooperation, the question will be how deep this partnership goes. Will the content of this partnership be a brief study tour or something more substantive?

In addition to traditional security concerns, a host of non-traditional security challenges will affect the UK and India. These include climate change, drug trafficking, infectious diseases, migration, disasters, resource scarcity and transnational crime. Whether the UK would be India's partner of choice in any of these could be a moot point. Had the UK wanted to work with India on any of these issues, or subsets of these issues, it could have done so at any point in the last decade. Earlier this year, for instance, France and India launched the International Solar Alliance, a financing programme aiming to lower the cost of solar power and to facilitate more than USD 1 trillion to members of the alliance. The UK has seemed reluctant to be the first-mover in forging such large-scale initiatives with India.

Further, the UK appears to have something of a scattergun approach, announcing during each visit an array of new ideas, many of which turn out to be limited in ambition. The Mumbai–Bangalore Economic Corridor springs to mind. Better would be to focus on a more limited number of issues and do them well. If the UK has chosen to help develop three smart cities—Pune, Amaravati and Indore—under the Smart Cities initiative, why is it redeveloping Varanasi railway station?

The choice lies with the UK rather than India. The UK is not the only country seeking to deepen its relationship with India and instead of looking at UK–India relations as an abstract subject, the UK would be better advised to look at it in comparison with other countries, some of which are investing heavily (financially) to improve relations. And the UK's 'shared historic ties', often mentioned, do not necessarily count in its favour.

India has set out its developmental priorities and its security concerns. With its youthful population, its economic growth is set to continue. The obvious issue that lies at the intersection of India's requirements and the UK's strengths is education—whether vocational certification or tertiary education. If the UK remains reluctant to meet India's clear request for easier visa access and to ease access for Indian students, it will be the UK's loss and its competitors' gain.

Gareth Price is a Senior Research Fellow at Chatham House.

India–UK Cultural Ties—Unlocking their Global Potential

Baroness Usha Prashar

The United Kingdom and India are both undergoing a shake-up of old political and social certainties.

The United Kingdom, one of the most prosperous countries in the world, is going through tumultuous change and uncertainty following its decision to leave the European Union. The full impact of this decision is yet to unfold. Many certainties have been shaken and the aftershocks are continuing. But there is no doubt this decision will have a profound effect on the United Kingdom's relationship with Europe and the world.

Whatever one may think of the rejection by the British electorate of membership of the European Union, it is a wake-up call. It cannot be dismissed as simply an outpouring of populism. Fear of migration has induced xenophobia. Globalisation, accelerating technological change, the global spread of the internet and social media, the threat of terrorism and widening inequality are leading people to look for a different deal.

How the UK reacts to these events will define the future.

Today's world is unpredictable. Competition is intense. We live in an age where the nature of conflict is changing fast. There is competition for scarce and finite resources. States are competing for influence. According to the

'Soft Power 30' survey compiled by Portland in partnership with Facebook, in 2016 the UK slipped to second place.

The report, which was published before the referendum on EU membership, said that Britain's high ratings reflect its 'enviable position at the heart of a number of important global networks' but it added that, 'in this context, a risk exists that the UK's considerable soft power clout would be significantly diminished should it vote to leave the EU'.

Post-referendum it is all the more necessary that the UK engages meaningfully with the world. This means adjusting to new realities which will require a different attitude, a new narrative and constant explanation. This has to be fully embraced if the UK is to reposition itself.

More than at any time in our history there is a need to work together and not turn inwards. There is a need to break down barriers within and between nations. There is a need to understand the nature and the extent of the change and respond to it with ingenuity and humility. While this is necessary in the light of Brexit, it is also necessary due to significant geopolitical and social shifts that have been taking place.

The point was well made by Lord Howell of Guildford in a lecture he gave at the Global Strategy Forum in 2014. He said, 'In a world of dispersed power, cloud information stores and e-enabled non-state threats, new instruments and techniques of influence and persuasion are required to underpin security and prevent the exercise of hostile forces. We need camaraderie, warmth and mutual respect.'

Following the referendum, the need for new instruments and techniques of influence and persuasion is greater than ever.

The UK will need to define and, in some instances, redefine its relationship with the wider world and its future direction. It needs to build on its vast reservoir of soft power: Its language, its literature—not only Shakespeare but JK Rowling, who is adored by young people in some Asian countries—and above all, its values. In an age of anxiety and uncertainty, the values the UK espouses are needed more than ever. As Churchill said, 'The empires of the future are the empires of the mind'. It is mindsets which need to be changed.

The UK's association with India is long and deep. Seventy years since India's independence, the world has changed and India too is changing and changing fast. Under Prime Minister Modi, India's engagement with the world is being transformed.

It is, therefore, necessary to reassess the relationship with India—necessary not just in terms of trade and investment but in the wider interests of the enormous challenges facing the world today.

Building a deeper understanding and putting the relationship on a more strategic footing, both the countries stand to benefit and could together become a formidable force for good in the world.

Both the UK and India have enormous soft power resources at their disposal, which if deployed with sensitivity and creativity could make a spectacular contribution to repositioning this relationship.

Prime Minister Modi is mobilising India's extensive soft power globally— a strategy which has been termed 'universal engagement'. India is engaging across the board and is deploying its soft power to build diplomatic and political relations. This is the first time India is taking systematic steps to spread its influence abroad.

India is recognised as the world's largest democracy. It is the birthplace of Mahatma Gandhi, the proponent of 'ahimsa', India's non-violent struggle for freedom. India's philosophical thought, spirituality, Ayurveda, yoga, arts, music, diverse cultures and heritage are its true treasures. Exotic foods, contemporary cinema—Bollywood—and music are part of its popular culture. The Indian diaspora is crucial to India's soft power, not least in disseminating and popularising Indian culture, tradition and cuisine. Indian food has made inroads globally and has been transformed and absorbed into several cuisines in the world. Gyms globally use Bollywood music in their fitness regimes. Yoga is widely practised and India remains a popular spiritual destination.

Promoting India as a spiritual place and a place of spiritual healing gives it a positive image. Declaring 21 June as World Yoga Day is a case in point. Sushma Swaraj speaking on World Yoga Day said:

> 'Yoga serves as a reminder of the potential for men and women to live in harmony with each other, as well as with nature, at a time when violent forces are threatening to destabilise society. Yoga is an important antidote to negativity— to move to the path of peace.'

Like the UK, India's soft power extends beyond arts and culture. Its democratic institutions, free press, independent judiciary, secularism, pluralism and rapid growth of information technology are its significant assets.

India is on a new path. It is embracing its position as a nation destined to be a significant world player. This transition could have significant consequences for the UK. India is already the third-largest economy in the world and is expected to become the second largest in the coming decades. Jim O'Neill, the well-known British economist, wrote, 'India will soon be one of the biggest influences in the world.'

India has shed the shadow of colonialism and is forging ahead with confidence. It is recalibrating its position to meet the challenges of future strategic realities.

This has vast implications for the future direction of India–UK relations: Historically a steady relationship, but one whose potential has not always been fully realised. It feels a little like the phrase of the great Indian poet, Rabindranath Tagore: 'I have spent many days stringing and unstringing my instrument, while the song I came to sing remains unsung.'

Against these new realities, what could be the future strategic nature and direction of this relationship and how can its full potential be realised?

Given the UK's and India's long and deep historical relationship, strong foundations are in place. For instance, the British Council opened its first Indian office in 1948 and is now in nine of India's major cities.

The two countries have a great deal in common and share an intricate relationship.

But like any relationship, with the passage of time and changing circumstances it needs to be reassessed and revitalised. Against the current realities, strengthening the strong cultural and economic relationship shared by the two countries is an imperative. Due to the forces of globalisation, India's commitments, interests and outlook require it to focus on more than the UK. The world is India's oyster. The UK no longer has a special place at the table.

India's diaspora is a vast network with interests across the world. Despite the UK's large Indian diaspora community it is by no means the only one. The diaspora is currently estimated to number over 20 million and covers practically every part of the globe.

Nowadays a remarkable number of Indian students go abroad to the USA, Australia and New Zealand. Although some come to the UK, the competition is growing and the UK's immigration policies are creating a negative impact. Other countries are benefiting as a result. For example, Indians now form the second largest number of foreign students in universities in the USA.

The time has come to revitalise this relationship and put it on a new footing. To put it crudely, it is time to move away from just 'chicken tikka masala culture' to a deeper, more meaningful and substantive dialogue. While it is true that India and the UK have a lot in common and that this relationship is built on historical ties—democratic values of freedom, equality and rule of law, pluralism, as well as cultural and linguistic influences—this mantra now needs to be explored with new eyes. Cultural articulation, in its broadest sense, between the two countries could be deeper, more sophisticated and could build a relationship which is based on mutuality, respect, understanding and goodwill.

Such a relationship has the potential of making the two countries, in partnership, a formidable force for good in the world. They can come together as significant players within the Commonwealth and promote its values and worth. The Commonwealth may have been founded during the British Empire days, but the new Commonwealth came into being after India's independence and when as a republic India was accepted as a member of the Commonwealth.

At a practical level, the two countries can work together to streamline bureaucracy and public administration, look at financial sector reform and create an enabling commercial environment for vibrant trade and investment. Coming together to build the capacity of relevant institutions, collaborating on research and development, and building partnerships in significant educational areas would be mutually beneficial.

In the longer term, a more sophisticated approach is required—a strategy that recognises and accommodates the diversity of India and the UK and engages the young. Ignorance of modern India and today's Britain, particularly among the young, will jeopardise the building of this new relationship if steps are not taken now and the current mindset does not change.

A report, 'India Matters', published by the British Council in 2015 on

India–UK relationship said that 'there is a growing sense of frustration in India as some feel that the colonial mindset still lingers...India is still not perceived or treated as an equal.'

The most striking finding of the research was that while 74 per cent of young educated Indians said they knew 'a great deal' or 'a fair amount' about the UK, just 21 per cent of young people from the UK said the same about India.

This is a worrying finding. It is an indication that the potential of this relationship has not been exploited for mutual benefit. If 'mutuality' is to work, there has to be parity of knowledge and understanding among both the countries. There is the obvious sharing of democratic values and the English language. But less obviously, there is an increasingly mainstream approach to nature and the living world that arises out of British respect and understanding of what are, arguably, quintessentially Indian values.

The influence of Gandhi and the encounters of thinkers like EF Schumacher with Indian thought in the last century are bearing fruit today. A growing understanding of the interconnectedness of living things and what might be termed as *ecological karma* are shaping cultural and political discourse.

There is great deal to be said for 'yoga diplomacy', a subtle form of diplomacy, a rich thread running through the approach of people around the world to ways of living together, with an unmistakably Indian origin. But these need to be popularised much more among the young, not just in cosmopolitan cities and towns but across both countries. They should not remain the domain of the few.

Another finding of the report 'India Matters', was that the India–UK relationship is characterised, at least by some people, by nostalgia—on both sides. For older generations of Indians, the UK was part of the fabric of life as a recently departed colonial power. The institutions put in place over centuries and left functioning in a newly-independent India ensured the existence of a feeling that the model for Indian lawyers, parliamentarians and civil servants was 'over there' in London and Whitehall.

But nostalgia is not a strong foundation for a living, breathing relationship. And seventy years after Indian independence, by one measure the span of a complete human life, and major geopolitical shifts and consequent changes, a rethinking and revaluing of the relationship is both inevitable and essential.

Trade and economic connections will certainly be vital elements of any reshaped relationship between India and the UK. But just as important—perhaps even more so in the long run—is the cultural relationship and people-to-people understanding. It is this which will be one of the foundation stones of a long-term strategic relationship. Culture, broadly defined, is after all how most people-to-people relationships are conducted—the sharing of experiences and ideas through common cultural interests and understandings. This is the best basis for building trust.

The key to making India matter to the UK and the UK matter to India, a challenge set by the British Council's 'India Matters' report, is a newly-invigorated cultural strategy, developing a deeper and more meaningful cultural understanding between people, particularly the young.

The 2017 UK–India Year of Culture will provide a major opportunity for cultural exchange between the two nations—an opportunity to lay foundations for a deeper dialogue with the potential for more sustainable outcomes in the longer run.

The Year of Culture should not be seen as a one-year wonder, but the basis for a step change in establishing a new, dynamic partnership. The Year of Culture has three objectives: To celebrate the UK–India relationship and India's seventy years of independence; to reconnect the next generation of Indians with their UK counterparts; to inspire people and institutions to create a shared future.

Conversation, collaboration and co-production will be at the heart of all this activity, as will mutuality, that is, each side valuing, respecting and learning from each other.

The ultimate aim is to establish new creative networks and ensure that cultural exchange extends further than the usual cultural elites, reaching beyond metropolitan populations to the towns and countryside of India and the UK. It is essential that non-urban populations do not feel disconnected from the cultural opportunities available to city dwellers.

If we are to close a gap between the cultural 'haves' and 'have nots', we need to work hard at cultural connections. If we are to connect to such diverse sections of both our communities and particularly the young, we must do so through the technologies with which they are comfortable. There is a competition for the attention of young people and in this new world only the fittest means of cultural connections will survive. Our objective must, therefore, be to see the India–UK relationship firmly established in that category.

Rethinking and revaluing that friendship and relationship is an imperative in the self-interest of both nations. In so doing, not only will both countries benefit, they will also be able to exert a positive influence in the affairs of the world.

In the world there is a vast reservoir of goodwill towards the UK, its values and its culture. India is seen as a non-violent, pluralistic democracy with a benign influence and its values are largely seen as benevolent and spiritual. With such rich heritage on both sides, cultural exchange is the best means to undertake the exploration of ideas and approaches. Cultural approaches can be a model for other forms of collaboration: Political, and social, and on the world stage.

We now need to use all our cultural resources to create a basis of knowledge and understanding for the sake of our security, prosperity and peace. We need more, not less, interaction if we are to understand and preserve the best in the world. But the quality and depth of that interaction matters. The UK and India now have a golden opportunity to make a step change and put their relationship on a new strategic footing.

Looking back we might learn something from the beginnings of the British experience of India, when the first European merchants met a culture that both enamoured and seduced them, and astonished them with its sophistication and its long history. This early cultural exchange was eventually supplanted by less attractive forms, driven by colonial and entrepreneurial ambition. Perhaps now is the time to rediscover that first form of our connection, with its curiosity, openness and surprise—on both sides.

Baroness Prashar CBE is Deputy Chair of the British Council and an independent member of the House of Lords.

Leveraging the UK's Deep-rooted Indian Diaspora

CB Patel

The Indian diaspora in the UK and the Indian overseas community is the culmination of several waves of migration spanning centuries, and it is important, across generations, to acknowledge and revisit our country's migration history.

The role of the Indian diaspora in the context of the UK's multicultural policies will largely depend upon its collective strength in the UK and its connectivity with India.

India is already the third-largest economy in the world (when measured at purchasing power parity exchange rates) and is expected to become the second largest in the coming decades.

As India's economy transforms, her political, military and cultural powers are also bound to rise, elevating her to a twenty-first century superpower. It is only inevitable that her foreign and economic policies are becoming increasingly outward-looking and her search for new global partners is gathering momentum. And this provides a great opportunity for the UK, probably more so in view of the Brexit verdict.

Through a number of initiatives, the UK is certainly investing in India and vice versa but the two countries have relatively low levels of trade.

Both Britain and India could do more to increase trading opportunities at a faster pace. One of the issues that must be addressed to speed up trade is allowing easier travel between the UK and India.

The UK's immigration rules limiting the number of skilled migrants into the country to work for specific businesses (using Tier 2 visas) are an impediment to expanding trading links. Approximately 700 Indian companies have invested in the UK, generating around 100,000 jobs. So if Indian companies face restrictions to import much-needed skill and talent, it is bound to impact on the way they do business.

The number of Indian students studying in the UK has also been declining after the government restricted the use of post-work study visas. The Indian government should make better use of its citizens abroad while leveraging its foreign policy.

The Indian community in the UK and those wishing to visit the country for business and leisure have been crying out for reforms that will provide a fairer system similar to that offered to Chinese nationals. Recent figures show that the number of Indian visitors has stagnated at around 400,000 per annum while the percentage of Indian tourists globally has increased. This is a clear indication that the UK is failing to attract sufficient leisure and business visitors. A positive change will encourage their spending, investment and trade in the UK.

British Indians—A Profile

Amongst all the overseas Indians in developed countries, Britain has the oldest and, in a way, uniquely placed Indian diaspora. It numbers at least 1.5 million and is mainly concentrated in a trapezium—London in the south, Leeds in the north-east, Manchester in the north-west and Leicester and Birmingham in the East and West Midlands. This total area is approximately 7,300 sq miles. In the United States its number is over 3.5 million, but in a much larger country like the US, it is much more widespread.

Prime Minister Narendra Modi has visited some fifty Indian diaspora during his foreign tours and the most enthusiastic reception he received was at the Wembley Stadium in London on 13 November 2015. Manoj Ladwa, the lead organiser of the grand event, and his colleagues aptly chose Wembley to make the biggest statement of India–UK relations ever.

No wonder, the then British PM David Cameron publicly acknowledged that he wouldn't have received such a rousing welcome from so many people in the UK.

INTEGRATION OF BRITISH INDIANS

The integration of British Indians began in 1607 when three sailing ships reached Surat on the west coast in Gujarat. The traders became rulers in a very short span of time.

The first migrant to touch the shores of the UK was named Peter (from Surat) who was baptised by the Archbishop of Canterbury, London.

Historian Dr Kusoom Vadgama, however, says he was from Bengal. 'Peter was a young man about whom we know very little about except that he came from Bengal. Peter was offered by the Dutch East India Company to an English company while on their way to Burma. He wasn't called Peter then. On 22 December 1616, he was baptised in a church in the City of London, and the name was given to him by King James the First of England and Sixth of Scotland. We don't know what his original name was and other details. He was brought to the UK—officially the first person to have his arrival recorded in the UK. Then he was trained here to study Christianity, Latin and English. He was said to be quite a nice and clever boy. Soon after his baptism in a month or so perhaps, he went back to India and they were hoping he would spread the knowledge of Christianity, Latin and English in India but we know nothing about it.'

It is believed that in the earlier period the East India Company brought some Indians, mainly Parsis and Maharashtrians, to England to train them as interpreters and translators and make them aware of the British administration.

In the eighteenth and nineteenth centuries, Bengalis especially the *bhadralok*, including the ancestors of Gurudev Rabindranath Tagore and others like Raja Ram Mohan Roy were frequent visitors to the UK and stayed in the island nation for some time. And then there was Srinivasa Ramanujan from Madras who did pioneering work in mathematics at Trinity College, Cambridge. He had almost no formal training in math, but is recognised as one of the greatest mathematicians of his time.

During that time several rajas, maharajas, nawabs and even landlords bought residencies on the south coast of Brighton and various other parts of the UK, especially London.

The Nawab of Rampur had bought 74 acres of land in the nineteenth century and now it is a thickly-populated residential area with two-thirds hailing from Indo-centric backgrounds. In the same period many merchants and shippers from Calcutta and other parts of the Bengal Presidency often visited England and some even settled there.

In the English law of contract, there is a famous case of Regazzoni v KC Sethia, a prominent jute businessman settled in Golders Green in north London. His fourth and fifth-generation descendants are settled here and are equally well known. In Manchester and London there were a large number of Indians—some Parsis and several Gujaratis who were engaged in textile trade and textile mills in Bombay and particularly Ahmedabad, which is known as the Manchester of India.

EDUCATION AND THE PROFESSIONS

Over the years more and more Indians came to the UK from India for Indian Civil Service and careers in law and medicine. Most of the leaders of the Indian Independence Movement—Mahatma Gandhi, Jawaharlal Nehru, Sardar Patel and MA Jinnah, to name a few—were trained as barristers in London. These leaders were deeply influenced by the liberal education they had received in the UK. The non-violent nature of the Indian Independence Movement resulted not only in the peaceful departure of the British from India but also helped in continuation of ties with the UK.

In 1919, Lord Satyendra Prasanno Sinha was appointed to the House of Lords—perhaps the first Indian—from Bengal Province.

The House of Lords has a unique relationship with Indian-origin persons. Lord Pratap Chitnis was the first British Indian who was elevated to the House post-1947. He was the treasurer of the Liberal Democrats Party. At that time the party was very small and short of resources.

Today in the House of Lords the largest number of non-White members is from India—numerically speaking, over two dozen. Some of them are making a huge impact, representing either the three main political parties or as cross-benchers.

WAR EFFORT AND THE INDIANS IN BRITAIN

Participation of a large number of Indian soldiers in the two World Wars also created a special bond between the armed forces of the two countries. In WWI, 1.2 million Indians fought on the war front, mainly in the European mainland. Between 1916 and 1918, 150,000 Indian soldiers were stationed in the southern coast of England in Sussex and Kent. Near Brighton there is a special crematorium where Hindus and Sikhs were given their final rites. The place is called Chattri, where every year a dignified service is conducted in their memory.

Brighton Pavilion is another symbol of influence of Indians—especially in architecture and philanthropy.

During WWII, the total number of the Indian fighting force was 2.4 million and another 1.7 million were employed in war efforts in undivided India.

During the war the British India exchequer had lent £800 million at the 1940 value, besides huge sums from rajas, diwans and nawabs—some involuntarily and some under duress.

During WWI and WWII the Indian soldiers and officers who were brought to the UK were more or less discouraged from settling in the UK, the land for which they laid down their lives. But that was the imperial period.

After the independence of India and Pakistan, migration to Britain became more popular especially from Pakistan and particularly from Mirpur district—from the part of Kashmir occupied by Pakistan.

At that time in the UK, there was a huge shortage of manpower, especially in industries like rubber, plastics, foundries, woollen and textile mills, London transport and the National Health Service (NHS), and these manpower needs were filled to a large extent by Indians.

In Southall, there was a rubber factory owned by British veterans and they needed hard-working people. Needless to say, this opened the floodgates for the Indians.

By 1961, a political hue and cry prevailed on the UK government to pass the Commonwealth Immigrants Act, 1962. What was meant to shut the door opened the floodgates for the Indians. Thousands came because the British needed them to look after their transport, NHS, industry and commerce.

Very soon these single men were joined by their spouses and with the birth of their children a permanent settlement took place. They included Gujaratis, Punjabis and Tamils, mainly from Sri Lanka.

In 1947, there were, perhaps, less than 5,000 people settled in the UK from India. But by 1962-63 the number rose to hundreds of thousands.

Then the arrivals came from East Africa. In the early 1960s, the largest number of overseas Indians, mainly Gujarati settlements, were in East Africa (Kenya, Uganda and Tanganyika). The 'Wind of Change' in 1957 was followed by the independence of Tanganyika on 9 December 1961, which was eventually followed by the freedom of Uganda and Kenya. Majority of East African Asians had acquired British citizenships, thanks to the encouragement by Apa Saheb Pant, the then high commissioner of India in Kenya.

This was also welcomed by the British authorities as they needed East African Asians to continue to work and live in East Africa and keep their huge savings in British banks. In the 1960s and early 1970s when the British exchequer was facing scarcity of foreign exchange, perhaps one of the largest sterling deposits were from the Asians (with British passports) living in Africa.

With political changes in East Africa the trickle into the UK began with Tanzania-based British passport holders, but the policy of Africanisation by President Jomo Kenyatta of Kenya started virtually the exodus in 1968-69.

In 1972, Idi Amin, the irresponsible dictator of Uganda, expelled British Asians as well as other Indians from the African nation and consequently a substantial number arrived in the UK. Credit must be given to then British PM Edward Heath and his courageous government which greeted the Asians holding British passports with open arms (considering it as their moral and legal responsibility).

During 1976, Indians from Zimbabwe, Zambia and Mozambique made a beeline to the UK. Some also came from Aden.

It is interesting to observe the composition of British Indians. The largest number was from Gujarati and Punjabi (Sikh) stock. There were others from other parts of India who came as doctors, teachers and other professionals.

Punjabis had settled in western London, mainly in boroughs of Ealing and Southall, and West Midlands. Gujaratis settled in Brent, Harrow and Barnet in London and Leicestershire, Lancashire and Manchester.

Of all the immigrants to the UK in the last fifty years or so, Indians have done exceptionally well in education, as professionals, in business, commerce, arts, culture and academics.

Also, the British establishment recognised that a British Indian per se is law abiding and able to integrate easily with the mainstream. As far as investments are concerned, today British Indians contribute a lot more than the percentage of their population. Equally important is the inflow of investments from India which is larger than the total of all former colonies which gained independence after WWII.

In the foreseeable future Indo-British economic partnership has enormous scope for development. They have different and complementary skills. Britain needs entrepreneurs and skilled personnel, while India could do with British expertise in international finance and infrastructure project management. There are many other areas of mutual cooperation.

It is worthwhile to remember that in the beginning of the seventeenth century India was much more advanced than the UK. Up until 1842, India and China were far more ahead than Europe or even the USA in terms of international economic performance.

What has been achieved between 1947 and 2016 is an eye-opener. In the last sixty-nine years, in spite of all the challenges, both man-made and natural, India has almost succeeded in putting its house in order. The prediction that India would disintegrate or won't be able to manage itself has been proved wrong. Not only has India remained a united country (of the size of a subcontinent) but has also remained democratic and secular in spite of the painful legacy of several centuries of foreign domination. While the average Indian is moving up the scale economically, Indian MNCs have invested billions of pounds in commerce and industry in the UK and other countries. It is worth remembering that Indians have an upper hand in certain sectors of modern economy. And this is just the beginning. Unfortunately, centuries of subjugation does have an impact on the psyche and temperament of the populace.

We must also accept that not all of the legacy of the British Empire is on the negative side. English language, the rule of law, independence of judiciary, freedom of press and certain other Western values did India a world of good, combined with its own tradition and cultural heritage.

No one could have foreseen that at the beginning of the twenty-first century there would be over 1.5 million residents of Indian heritage in the UK.

Compared to their other British peers, British Indians are way ahead in education, entrepreneurship, savings and several other aspects of life.

The younger generation born and brought up in the UK with higher education and qualifications, combined with the traditional values, is forging ahead. Look at their numbers in prisons—just a miniscule percentage. Similarly, British Indians are respected for their peaceful and non-violent nature. Why is the younger generation of British Indians faring better in every walk of life? In large part, this must have something to do with the Indian tradition and values.

While the British government has not yet fully recognised the potential of this small yet talented mass of Indian diaspora, I fear the Indian government too has not yet developed strategies and structures to sustain the links with the upcoming generation of overseas Indians. For instance, except the Bharatiya Vidya Bhavan, there has been no Indian organisation in the UK which has evolved as a recognised and resourceful action-oriented institution to propagate the beauty of Indian culture and arts.

The younger Indian diaspora in modern-day Britain needs to be encouraged to enjoy the best of both worlds—i.e. to look at their roots and retain whatever is worthwhile and pick up the best from the British society too. That is true integration. Given this history and success, just perhaps, there may be lessons to be shared in the story of British Indians for other immigrant communities too. As the UK government grapples with growing concerns over migration, and as India flexes its muscles on the world stage, the history, experience and talents of British Indians, should be much better utilised.

CB Patel is the founder of Asian Business Publications Limited (ABPL), the UK-based media house behind *Asian Voice* and *Gujarat Samachar* news weeklies and the Asian Achievers Awards.

UNLEASHING THE GREAT INDIA–UK PARTNERSHIP

London Will Always Be At Forefront of India–UK Ties

Rt Hon Sadiq Khan

In my final year as an MP, I would often pass by the giant bronze sculpture of Mahatma Gandhi, which stands in London's Parliament Square, facing towards the Palace of Westminster. The statue of the man revered in India as the Father of the Nation, swaddled in a shawl and wearing a traditional dhoti with his hands clasped, is inspired by the iconic photographs that were taken of Gandhi during a visit to our capital in 1931, when he famously stood on the steps of 10 Downing Street after a meeting with the then Prime Minister Ramsay MacDonald to discuss Indian independence.

For me, Gandhi's permanent place in Parliament Square today alongside other towering figures of world politics, such as Winston Churchill and Nelson Mandela, serves as a potent reminder of the long history that binds our two nations together. His presence also speaks to the journey that both our countries—one of the world's oldest democracies and the largest—have been on.

The long-standing, centuries-old connections between Britain and India, which were originally forged on the basis of trade, remain etched into the landscape of modern London. While the West India Docks (now home to Canary Wharf) and the East India Docks (now a sanctuary for wildlife) are no longer operating, their legacy lives on in our city as they were once among the busiest docks in the world, importing tea, spices and various other Indian commodities.

But it isn't just the names of some of London's historic sites that shed light on the enduring ties that exist between India and our city. The stories of many of today's Londoners do too, not least my own which in many ways is bound up with the history of India–UK relations.

My grandparents were born in India but migrated to Pakistan following Independence. Shortly before I was born, my parents moved from Pakistan to London. They were part of a generation of immigrants from the Commonwealth who came to this country after the Second World War to help rebuild Britain's town and cities and fill labour shortages in our NHS and other essential public services.

When they arrived in London, my dad worked as a bus driver and my mum as a seamstress, stitching clothes to help make a bit of extra money for our family. Their adopted city and the city of my birth was incredibly kind to them. London gave my mum and dad a secure council house, which allowed them to save for a deposit so they could later buy a home of their own. London also gave me and my siblings the opportunities to fulfil our potential. We all benefited from a good state school education and afterwards my brother had access to a high-quality apprenticeship, while I was able to study law, thanks to affordable university tuition.

It goes without saying that I'm incredibly proud to be a Brit and a Londoner. This country and city have given my family and me far more than we could ever have dreamt of and I'm determined to repay that debt as mayor by working to improve the quality of life and life chances of all Londoners.

It's also true to say though that I remain keenly aware of my roots— both as a child of immigrants and as someone of South Asian heritage. These aspects of my identity mean I feel a deep affinity for the subcontinent and they perhaps help me more easily recognise the many things that we have in common.

As a truly global capital, London is one of the most diverse cities on earth. More than 300 languages are spoken on our streets and I'm confident you would struggle to find a nationality that isn't represented here. Similarly, India is a multi-ethnic, multi-linguistic, multireligious society that offers many lessons about how people from different faiths and backgrounds can be accommodated alongside one another.

It's apparent today both London and India value pluralism and that each subscribes to the idea of unity in diversity. In fact, I strongly believe that our diversity is one of our greatest strengths and so against this backdrop of common values, I want to build on our shared democratic and cosmopolitan culture to establish an even stronger relationship between our city and the State of India.

I think there is immense potential to deepen and expand our links across a wide range of fields, from business and the economy to tourism, higher education, clean energy and finance. Of course, our shared history, shared connections and shared values make this a natural partnership. But so too does the fact that London plays host to an enormous Indian diaspora community, numbering over 610,000 people—the largest of all the overseas populations living here in our capital.

This community has made a huge contribution to London's success over many decades and India, along with her neighbours, has arguably played as big a part as any in terms of shaping and enriching our capital's culture. Indian nationals, British Indians and second and third-generation immigrants who live in London today form the foundation of our city's unique friendship with the subcontinent and also mean that we are ideally positioned to cultivate further ties to our mutual benefit.

While in the past this has not always been the case, today the relationship between the UK and India is defined by reciprocity, equality and shared interests. It is one that in more recent years has strengthened both places and their economies, and which has been underpinned by exchange in multiple areas, from trade and inward investment to culture and migration. In my role as mayor of London, I want to support, facilitate and grow these bonds that draw us so closely together because I firmly believe that moving forward our city and India have much to gain from increased cooperation and partnership.

Nowhere is this truer than in the area of economic development. Today, London and India share a common vision for the future based on innovation, entrepreneurship and the creation of high-skill, high-wage economies that deliver rising prosperity for all Londoners and Indians. But while there are real economic rewards on offer to us both, these can only be maximised through genuine collaboration. Indeed, collaboration will be the guiding principle of the next phase of relations between London and India as my administration looks to mark a new chapter in this historic relationship.

Today, we are a long way from trading tea, cotton and spices. Indeed, for London and India it is now all about nurturing growth in the financial services, tech and life sciences sectors that are so vital to sustaining our knowledge-based economies. Increasingly our economic interactions are also taking place around smart cities, the financing of infrastructure and the development of new technologies that will help tackle the major environmental challenges of our time, such as climate change and air quality—two problems which pose as much of a threat to Londoners as they do to people living in Mumbai, Kolkata, Delhi, Chennai and Bengaluru.

For Indian business, London will continue to serve as the pre-eminent launch pad for entry into key markets—both in the UK and around Europe. That's because regardless of Brexit, the many benefits of operating a business with an international outlook from our city will remain. The fact that in London, companies can count on the availability of a highly-educated workforce, world-class professional and business services, the rule of law, unmatched connectivity, a favourable time zone, the English language and access to capital markets means our status as a critical hub of the global economy is assured.

Along with the ease of doing business in London and our reputation as one of the world's most cosmopolitan, inclusive and welcoming cities, these factors help to explain why Indian companies are already investing more in the UK than they do in the rest of the European Union combined, supporting some 110,000 jobs in our capital. They also explain why Indian conglomerates, such as ACG Europe Ltd, Infosys and the Tata group have chosen to base either their European headquarters or significant elements of their European operations in London.

Measured by total number of projects, India is the second-largest investor in London after the US. The country accounted for 11 per cent of all foreign direct investment projects in London from 2005 to 2016, creating around 5,000 new jobs. This very much mirrors the national picture, as over the same period India invested more in the UK than any other country except the US. But there is no room for complacency because others are trying to steal a march on the UK and lure greater amounts of Indian investment to their own countries.

In recent years, we have seen a big movement towards Germany following a concerted push by its diplomats and businesses to court Indian investors. At the same time, there has been a sense among some Indian business leaders that while successive British governments might talk a good game on British–Indian trade, their actions do not always live up to their rhetoric. We must work to address this perception and ensure that we are delivering on our words because Indian investment is extremely important for our national economy and London's too.

Notably, a high proportion of the inward investment currently coming into London from India is in the tech sector. In fact, nearly half (46 per cent) of all Indian investment pouring into our city today goes into tech. This is largely because London has been able to distinguish itself as the obvious choice for Indian tech firms looking to build their reach into Europe and globalise their businesses. But while Nesta and the European Digital Forum's city index have named our city as the best in Europe for start-ups and scale-ups, we must not rest on our laurels.

London's promotional agency, London & Partners, is ensuring we remain a magnet for Indian tech investment through initiatives like the India Emerging Twenty (IE20) competition, which aims to identify India's twenty most innovative and high-growth companies with global aspirations. The winners will visit during London Technology Week 2017 as part of a unique programme that will help their businesses develop their global potential though various mentoring, match-making and networking opportunities.

The competition is designed to help Indian companies establish a footprint in London, allowing them to grow, expand and find new markets, while simultaneously promoting their brand and raising their profile. Since being chosen for last year's programme, a number of companies have already attracted investment and set up shop in London, including Teabox, Kyazoonga and Seclore, all of whom received venture capital funding.

I'm proud to say the investment is flowing both ways though, with exciting new opportunities emerging for London firms to partner with Indian cities, amid recent commitments by the UK businesses to make £2 billion worth of investments in the country over the next five years. The rise of India's sizeable English-speaking middle class also means in the decades ahead, our creative industries are set to export more of their output than ever before to the subcontinent. The Indian appetite for blockbuster films, such as JK Rowling's *Fantastic Beasts and Where to Find Them*, which was filmed on the streets of London, will only grow exponentially in the near future, while simultaneously the Indian film industry and Bollywood can expect to find new audiences among Londoners.

What's clear to me is that there is massive scope for London's companies to engage with and tap the potential of India's widening consumer base in the coming years. As mayor, I will do everything in my power to support those London firms seeking to unlock this market and export their products and services to India. Our business community has much to offer Indian consumers and is perfectly placed to continue London's long tradition of being open to sharing ideas and trading with other nations from around the world.

We are fortunate in London to be home to some of the best and brightest minds, as well as some of the top global talent in the nascent big data, mobility and sustainability sectors. Many of these individuals hail from India or are from Indian backgrounds originally and alongside other members of our global workforce, they are helping to devise and test innovative solutions that stand to not only make our city more efficient, cleaner and greener but also boost our economy.

Some of this innovation, much of which is focused on smart technologies and renewable energy, is already spreading overseas, including back to India. This trend is only likely to accelerate following the announcement of India's Smart Cities Mission by Prime Minister Narendra Modi in June 2015. The creation of 109 smart cities, which represent a £24 billion investment opportunity, is an excellent chance to reinforce the partnership between London and India. To date, the UK has already partnered with three of the initial twenty lighthouse cities—Pune, Amaravati and Indore—which together are anticipated to invest up to £4.8 billion in infrastructure, energy and urban services over the next five years. I want London's business to be at the forefront of such projects and so we are ready to explore any meaningful opportunities for partnerships that may arise.

I'm aware though that for London to be in a position to seize such opportunities it must remain open to talent. Indian tech firms, as well as those from the United States, East Asia and of course Europe, will only locate to London if they are sure they can call on workers with the necessary skill sets. This is an argument I regularly make to the UK government because I know that the only way London can maintain its competitive edge is by protecting its ability to attract first-rate talent from across the globe.

But work is not the only reason why so many talented Indians decide to travel to London. Our city's institutions of higher education are incredibly popular among Indians, who comprise the third-largest group of international students. Whether they opt to stay put following their studies to contribute their skills and knowledge to our world-class life sciences, finance or professional services sectors, or choose to return home, and in doing so become ambassadors abroad for our city and country, strengthening the bonds between our economies, I'm passionate about making Indian students feel welcome in London.

However, there is no escaping the harsh reality that the number of Indian students studying in London has declined considerably in the last four years—partly due to the removal of the post-study work visa. I believe the UK government has got it badly wrong on this issue and as a result dissuaded many prospective Indian students from applying to study in our country. One of my biggest concerns in the wake of the EU referendum vote continues to be the impact it could have on our higher education sector. In my view, it is absolutely crucial that foreign students who want to study in London are able to do so, because they are crucial for our economy. My ambition therefore is to see many thousands more Indians follow in the footsteps of Mahatma Gandhi, Jawaharlal Nehru and Bhimrao Ambedkar, all of whom studied here.

I also want the message to be heard far and wide that London remains open to Indian tourists. Our city is one of the most popular in the world to visit and is presently attracting record numbers of international tourists.

Tourism supports 700,000 jobs in our capital and is worth £36 billion to London's economy every year so it is imperative that it continues to thrive. In 2015, Indians made 276,000 visits to London, spending over £200 million, while over the last five years there has been a 17 per cent increase in the numbers visiting and a 22 per cent increase in their spending. And they leave with great memories of London. As mayor, I appreciate I have a responsibility to help continue this positive trend and so alongside London & Partners, I will do everything in my power to promote London and its amazing attractions to international and Indian tourists.

But London is not only somewhere for Indians to visit, study and grow their tech businesses; it is also a place where their country can access finance to fund infrastructure spending. Over £900 million (INR 7,500 crore) of rupee-denominated bonds have been issued in London since July 2016, cementing London's status as the leading global centre for offshore rupee finance. For example, India's Housing Development Finance Corporation issued a bond worth £366 million—the first ever masala bond to be issued outside of India—while the National Thermal Power Corporation issued another worth £244 million. These transactions have paved the way for Indian corporates to raise significant sums in London. And I hope, indeed expect, these to be just the first in a string of such offerings after the Indian PM signalled his backing for over £1 billion worth of private sector masala bonds to be issued in London when he visited in late 2015.

I'm in no doubt that London and the UK will remain in pole position when it comes to financing India's growth and the modernisation of its infrastructure. So far, as many as thirty offshore Indian rupee bonds have been listed on the London Stock Exchange—including, last year, the listing of the world's first-ever green masala bond, which seeks to leverage private sector investment to address climate change in India. These bond issues continue to reinforce confidence in London as the focal point of global financial markets—following as it does the launch of several bonds in London denominated in Chinese renminbi, as well as Islamic bonds, known as sukuk. Even post-Brexit, this unique service cannot simply be replicated elsewhere or transferred overnight, as it is founded on decades of building mutual trust in our city's economic institutions and financial law.

While the result of the EU referendum was not the one that I, or indeed the majority of Londoners had hoped for, Britain is now on course to leave the EU. I regret that, and I'm sure that view will be shared by Indian business interests in London, but we must deal with the situation as it is, not as we might wish it to be. And so I note that following the EU referendum, India was among the first countries to express an interest in agreeing to a bilateral trade deal with the UK at the earliest opportunity. I will press the UK government to make sure a trade deal with India is a high priority.

The prospect of such an agreement is, I believe, a reflection of our close economic ties as well as the friendship between our two countries. Throughout my mayoralty, I pledge to do whatever I can to further strengthen and develop that friendship because I know that across our country, especially in London, Indians and the Indian diaspora have made an absolutely vital contribution to our economic and cultural life. And while I cannot speak for the whole of the UK, what I can say on behalf of London is that we will always be open to India and the Indian people.

Sadiq Khan is the Mayor of London.

.

Past, Present and Future—The Changing Tide of India–UK Economic Relations

LORD MEGHNAD DESAI

Trade and economic relations between India and the UK are more than 400 years old. From 1600, when the East India Company began trading, there have been several distinct phases. The first phase, with the English buying exportables in India and using Indian ports as entrepôt for their trade in Southeast Asia, lasted 150 years. In this phase, India was the destination of many European nations wishing to trade, as India, along with China, was where the wealth was. Asia enjoyed a trade surplus which had to be settled in gold. There was a big controversy in England and elsewhere in Europe about this drain of gold. The mercantilists argued that trade should always yield a surplus for the home country.

Then in the mid-eighteenth century, two things happened which altered the power relations. East India Company moved into the political vacuum created by the decline of Mughal power and took over several parts of India starting with Bengal and Carnatic (today's Tamil Nadu). It took the company ninety years (1757-1847) to complete its conquest of India. But independent of this campaign, the Industrial Revolution occurred in Great Britain which altered the economic power relation between the two. Before the late eighteenth century when the Industrial Revolution took place, per capita incomes were similar across the world. Countries like China and India were richer because they had a larger population. However, Great Britain was now able to produce textiles at much lower prices than any other country. India became a net buyer of textiles (and other manufactured products) from the early nineteenth century onwards. It exported agricultural goods now. The alteration in the economic power relationship affected not just India but many countries in Europe as well as countries of Asia before they could catch up with Great Britain in the industrial race. China fell behind just like India did though it was not conquered by any European power. It was defeated in the Opium Wars and later had to accept unequal treaties with Western powers and cede sovereignty in its ports.

The Company was replaced by the Crown for the next ninety years following the 1857 War of Independence. Now India was shaped into an administrative unit with fledgling modern industries such as railroad, textiles and others. India continued to be treated as a raw material exporting country though slowly manufacturing units were started by Indian entrepreneurs along with British businesses, as for example, in jute textiles.

India was enfeebled by the displacement from industrial leadership after the Industrial Revolution and the discouragement from the metropolitan power. Only during the two World Wars did India develop modern industry. Even so it was the junior partner in trade. Its export surplus provided surplus sterling balances for the home country's reserves and buoyed up the pound sterling. But it was overcharged for home stores etc. which was denounced by the Indian nationalists as a drain.

The imperial experience convinced the Indian nationalists that they had to industrialise India when it became independent and that they should not just rely on foreign trade.

China had a chequered period in the twentieth century. The Empire under the Qing dynasty broke up and China became a republic in 1911. It was still a backward country in terms of economic strength. The interwar period failed to establish a strong national government and then China suffered Japanese invasion. Being independent rather than a British colony did not help China. In 1949, the Communist Party led a revolution and the Guomindang under Chiang Kai-shek's leadership retreated to Taiwan. At this time of the revolution, the levels of per capita income were the same in India and China.

INDEPENDENCE AND AFTER (1947-1990)

From 1947 till the end of the century, India continued to be an importer and recipient of FDI from the UK. Great Britain was a leading country in giving foreign aid to India, including the steel plant at Bhilai. India exported skilled and unskilled labour and a diaspora was built up in the process. India had political weight in the Commonwealth but not much economic clout. It industrialised but relied too much on the public sector and tried to become self-sufficient. Heavy tariffs were imposed on imports and the entry of foreign capital was discouraged. The domestic private sector was restrained by permits and licenses. India grew but at a very slow pace. Fair to say, some of these ideas of State intervention and controls had been imported from the British Labour Party and its thinking, especially Fabian socialism. But while the UK moved on under Margaret Thatcher and converted itself into a dynamic market economy, India clung to its old beliefs.

China also tried to industrialise, using Soviet methods. Mao was also given to extreme targets and overextension of the economy. This caused one of the biggest famines, killing 40 million people. China also went through a cultural revolution which wrecked the economy. When Mao died in 1975, India and China had the same per capita incomes. The UK recognised the People's Republic of China soon after 1949 as its legitimate government while USA did not.

It was after 1978 that China took off under Deng Xiaoping's leadership. Since then China has grown at double-digit rate and has quadrupled its GDP. It has grown by developing manufacturing industry and has used its extensive supply of cheap labour and its own savings (at the rate of 50 per cent in households) to become a formidable presence.

INDIA RESURGENT (1991-2016)

It is in the last twenty-five years since the Rao–Singh economic reforms that the situation has been transformed. India cut its tariffs and relaxed quotas. Private sector was released from restrictions. Foreign capital was made welcome. India began to thrive in the services sector, especially IT. It began to export IT services abroad in large amounts. Companies such as Infosys and Wipro made their global presence felt.

Then during the first decade of the twenty-first century, India became an exporter of capital. Indian businesses were able to buy out companies abroad. The diaspora—NRIs—collaborated with Indians in capturing and running many businesses. From being a weak trading partner in the nineteenth and twentieth centuries, India has emerged as a potential powerhouse in the twenty-first. Now there are Indian-owned companies abroad. There are Indians occupying CEO positions in leading multinationals—Microsoft, Google, Lego.

Recent headlines in the UK have been about Tata Steel and its decision to continue or shut its Welsh plant. This was a result of the Tata purchase of British Steel which had become Corus after its sale to a Dutch company. The idea that the decisions of the Tata board sitting in Mumbai would determine the fate of thousands of Welsh workers would have been unthinkable just fifteen years ago. Here was a multinational, originating in India, holding the future of thousands of British workers in its control.

This latest phase of Indo-UK trade and economic relations is thus much more a story of give and take on an equal footing. India is not just a market for British goods or a destination for investment, it is also a major investor in the UK and a trading partner. With Tata's purchase of Jaguar Land Rover and its success as a dynamic exporting company, India's role in the British economy has been altered completely.

The major Chinese investment in the UK is in nuclear reactors for energy generation. In collaboration with France's EDF group, Chinese suppliers will build two nuclear reactors for electricity generation.

BREXIT UK

The UK economy has come well through the recession, registering one of the highest growth rates of GDP among the G7. But the Brexit decision has injected a lot of uncertainty about its future. As the UK withdraws from the EU, it is uncertain as to what the framework of its future relations with the EU27 will be. It will be 2020 before we know. But at the same time, the UK will have to join the WTO once it exits EU and negotiate free trade agreements with the rest of the world. India, China and the emerging economies will be at the forefront of the UK's wish list as its preferred partners for future trading relations.

This is likely to give India a strong bargaining position. India wants to continue to send students to the UK universities and its skilled workers to the UK companies. This is a tough demand for the UK as the major motivation for Brexit was the control of immigration. India will have to bargain strongly for its core demand. India also invests in the UK and would want to continue to do so. The UK invests in India and exports goods and services. It wants to be able to export legal services to India which India has been resisting for the last several years. The UK also wants the City of London to be able to pitch more financial services to India. This may be easier for India to grant rather than legal services penetration by the UK.

The main agenda item in the near future—the next five years—will be the shape of the UK–India FTA. As India is growing at a fast rate, it will become more versatile. Its exports of goods and services as well as skilled labour will grow. The UK is also a strong service export nation, especially in higher education. If immigration to the UK becomes a sticky point, then the UK universities can locate to India and/or set up distance learning/online facilities. The demand for quality higher education in India is most incredibly high and growing fast. India would also welcome the UK investment as part of its Make in India initiative. In recent years, the UK has lost its edge to France and Russia in selling defence equipment. It will have to work hard to regain it.

The Future

There is no doubt that India–UK economic relations will stay close and strong. But over the years, India has reduced the economic distance between the UK and itself. As the fastest-growing economy with a favourable demography, India has every chance of becoming one of the three richest countries along with USA and China. Of course in per capita terms it will be a middle-income country for the next twenty-five years. The UK will remain a high-income economy, among the G7. Its trade with India will contain items of soft power—literature, arts, theatre, films, music—as much as goods and services. It is also a highly innovative economy as its progress in fintech shows. British universities are research and development hubs and India has a lot to learn from the UK in this respect.

It is worth comparing India with China in this respect. During the last five years, China has become a major investor in the UK. The proposal to build nuclear power reactors at Hinkley Point to supply electricity in the future has been taken up by China. When George Osborne was chancellor (2010-2016), he was very active in seeking Chinese investments. The City of London has been helping China with its RMB bonds, a much bigger business than the masala bonds India has floated. More recently, China is reported to have scaled down its resort to the city for RMB bonds. China is also facing problems on both household and corporate non-performing loans.

It is a moot point as to whether China's role will grow or shrink over the next few years. The Chinese economy is slowing down in those sectors where it was a lead producer-cum-exporter. China is now more reliant on its domestic consumer for growth. India can fill in some gaps because China may lose out to other Western countries. China is becoming much more dependent on a few large firms because decision-makers fear American technological power. China is dependent on local aggregate demand rather than exportable goods and services.

India specialises in medium-tech manufacturing such as automobile parts and pharmaceuticals. It is much more advanced in the services sector. China has specialised in low-tech manufacturing but recently developed R&D-intensive sectors as well. The UK will need trading partners both as markets and as suppliers and investors. As China transits from its manufacturing export base to its domestic consumer market sector, it may be less of a rival to India. There is also the advantage India has over China, that in English it enjoys a pivotal soft power activity. In education, culture, arts and tourism, India has a comparative advantage which it should be able to exploit.

India will continue to make its presence felt in the British economy as Tata Steel and Jaguar Land Rover have already done. Indian entrepreneurs will take over more companies in the UK. As time passes it will be India which will be the stronger economy with a greater potential than the UK in the partnership. It is the UK which needs and will need even more of India's skill and resources than the other way around. The UK economy will take five to ten years to fully adjust to the post-Brexit equilibrium. Within that time India will have made up even more ground. The story of the UK–India economic relationship may go back to what it was in 1600.

Lord Desai is Emeritus Professor of Economics at the London School of Economics.

New Sparks Needed to Unleash India–UK Partnership

Lord Jitesh Gadhia

India's Prime Minister Narendra Modi is well known for sharing his thoughts and ideas directly with millions of Indians through his inspirational radio programme *Mann Ki Baat* (Matters of the mind). However, for two great democratic nations like India and Britain, with such a deep-rooted relationship, there should also be *Dil Ki Baat* (Matters of the heart).

For those of us from the UK, who have a long-standing interest in strengthening our partnership, I would say: *Yeh Dil Maange More* (Our hearts want more). We really do want more and closer engagement with India and there could not be a more opportune moment to intensify our collaboration, particularly on bilateral trade, investments and capital flows.

I had the privilege of working closely with Britain's former Prime Minister David Cameron who, I believe, did more than any other holder of his position to build a modern partnership with India. I am, therefore, pleased that our new Prime Minister, Theresa May, is building on this strong legacy and, like her predecessor, chose India for her first major planned official visit overseas.

In doing so, both of them identified a common cause—harnessing an 'aspiration nation'. If you believe that demography determines destiny, then India, with more than half its population under the age of twenty-five years, is the ultimate place to capture the benefits of scale, consumption growth and capital formation on a magnitude unrivalled in human history. That will make India one of the key engines of global growth in the coming decades, along with China and the US.

FRIENDS IN NEED

Amidst all the noise surrounding Brexit, the Trumpification of the US, the brave demonetisation move by Prime Minister Modi, as well as the perennial vexed issues of migration, students and visas, let us not forget the fundamentals that now define our relationship. It is no exaggeration to say that we are at a defining moment in British history as we grapple with the new realities outside the European Union. We stand at a crossroads for the UK and its future relationship with the rest of the world.

If Britain wants to pursue the India opportunity, then it must reach out to India more confidently and aggressively. Like any attractive bride, India is being courted actively by multiple suitors. The next generation of Indians—the children of independent India—don't share the same historical and emotional ties with Britain. This generation is looking to the US.

The UK needs to get inside the psyche of young and modern India. It can do so by identifying shared interests that address the most pressing challenges for India and match them with the biggest strengths of the UK. At the same time, I hope that India will reach out to the UK and recognise both the necessities and the opportunities opened up by its negotiated departure from the European Union. As the saying goes, 'a friend in need is a friend indeed'.

UNLOCKING THE TRADE IMPASSE

The UK will clearly need to demonstrate some 'quick wins' as it seeks bilateral trade deals outside the current EU multilateral framework. Meanwhile, the EU–India FTA is at an impasse where talks have been going on ever since 2007. I believe this opens up a golden opportunity for India to push both parties hard for securing ambitious trade deals across multiple fronts.

If you look at Britain's history, it is a trading nation first, last and always—so I am confident that there will be a UK–India trade treaty sooner than one with the EU. Although an actual treaty cannot be signed until Britain leaves the EU, there could certainly be an interim stage of signing a memorandum of understanding, which can be achieved before then.

However, the UK will be capacity constrained in running too many parallel trade processes—I am told that the practical number is no more than four or five—and therefore playing 'too cute' might mean that the British priority shifts elsewhere.

INVESTMENT TRUMPS TRADE

While the trade bandwagon gets rolling, the bilateral investment flow will no doubt continue apace, much as it has done during the last decade. I have had the privilege of leading some of the largest investment flows between the UK and India, ranging from steel to pharmaceuticals. This experience has provided valuable insights into both the immense potential as well as the pitfalls.

Indeed, the depreciation in the sterling exchange rate post Brexit has arguably done more for the UK inward investment than any government intervention or incentives could ever achieve. At prevailing exchange rates, with sterling reaching a thirty-one-year low against the dollar, Indian companies should find the acquisition of the UK businesses and assets attractive, particularly if they take a medium-term strategic view, which looks beyond the current uncertainty.

Taking this longer-range perspective is exactly what the Ahmedabad-based global generics company, Intas Pharmaceuticals, has done with its £600 million acquisition of Actavis UK & Ireland announced in October 2016, creating a leading generics player in the UK. It represents the largest Indian investment into the UK since Brexit and is a vote of confidence in the future of the British economy.

Above all else, the UK and India should focus on providing a stable, consistent and predictable business environment. All the empirical evidence shows that inward investment is highly correlated to these features.

OPEN TO INVESTMENT BUT NOT MIGRATION AND STUDENTS?

We should acknowledge, though, that the issue of migration and visas has clouded the perceptions about the UK's continuing openness for both business and overseas students.

My personal experience is that Britain is an open and tolerant society which welcomes people from all over the world who can make a contribution to the country. Our new Prime Minister, Theresa May, speaks of making Britain a great meritocracy, a place where advantage is based on merit not privilege; where it's your talent and hard work that matter, not where you were born; who your parents are or what your accent sounds like.

While we witnessed some unfortunate rhetoric and emotions stirred during the Brexit debate, I hope these will subside over time. We do have to recognise the origins of these sentiments and tackle the root cause—which lies in alienation of people left behind by the forces of globalisation. This is an international phenomenon not just isolated to Britain or the US; the European elections during 2017—in the Netherlands and Germany—may yet provide some more surprises.

To use some literary analogies from Jane Austen's books, I am confident that Britain will remain the land of 'Sense and Sensibility' rather than 'Pride and Prejudice'. We should therefore retain a sensible and welcoming approach to attracting bona fide Indian students and high-skilled workers to our shores.

For millions of Indians, education is seen as the way out of poverty. Indian parents spend an estimated USD 13.5 billion annually in educating their children abroad. The UK visa regime permitting, British universities have a unique opportunity to attract more students from India as well as set up campuses in India under proposed legislation. The UK government should redouble efforts to make clear that there are no limits on student numbers. It should also review the process of granting overseas students the right to work in Britain after graduation and enable British companies to recruit fresh graduates directly from Indian universities and train them in the UK. This focus on education will generate a long-term shared prosperity built across generations. The impact on the sentiment of 'young India' would be deep.

Beyond higher education, there would be a huge thirst for vocational skills from the 270 million Indians who would be entering the workforce over the next twenty years. India needs a skilled workforce that is measurable and mobile if it is to retain an edge over China as a value-added manufacturer. Britain benefits a lot from globally-recognised training standards and qualifications. Tata's investments in British steel and car manufacturing, which now make the Indian conglomerate the largest industrial employer in the UK, is a powerful recognition of British manufacturing technical skills and training.

BOOSTING INFRASTRUCTURE AND CAPITAL FLOWS

Having spent the last twenty-five years involved with a number of major global financial institutions, I would highlight the important—and still underdeveloped role—which the UK can play in financing India's economic development.

As well as building human capital, India also has ambitious plans to invest over USD 830 billion on physical infrastructure over the next five years (2017-2022) including power, roads, railways, ports and airports to support the inexorable urbanisation of India. The capacity to deliver on this scale of investment depends crucially on forging public–private partnerships and accessing innovative financing—a mission for which India's National Investment and Infrastructure Fund (NIIF) has being established. British architects, transport consultants, civil engineers, contractors, equipment manufactures and project financiers now have an opportunity to build large swathes of twenty-first century India—the so called 'Smart Cities'—just as an earlier generation did in the nineteenth century.

Completing the trio of human and physical capital is, of course, the financial capital. With a common language and legal structures, and favourable time zone, the City of London remains the obvious gateway for Indian companies wanting to access global financial markets. Unlike China, which is a growing exporter of capital requiring an offshore renminbi centre, India will continue to require inward investment flows.

London remains officially ranked as the world's number one financial centre. We are home to over 250 foreign banks—more than any other centre. Over 500 foreign companies are listed on the London Stock Exchange and over 40 per cent of the world's foreign exchange transactions take place in the city. In fact, more US dollars are traded in London than in New York.

The UK-based fund managers invest over £6 trillion in assets, which is almost five times the size of the Indian economy, which has supported the development of the nascent masala bond market. In the twelve months since Prime Minister Modi spoke about 'James Bond, Brooke Bond and Rupee Bond' during his widely acclaimed speech at Wembley Stadium in November 2015, we have seen London raise USD 4 billion through thirty-two rupee bond issues to invest in Indian infrastructure, making Britain the leading centre. We have also seen HDFC issue the world's first Indian corporate masala bond.

However, this is only the start and we have the ability to mobilise further capital and financial expertise: To invest in India's infrastructure alongside NIIF; to issue bonds or equity for India's companies; to insure their risks—with Lloyds of London having recently received permission to operate onshore; to hedge currency or commodity exposures and to provide the world's best professional services network ranging from accounting to legal services. In summary, I truly believe there is no better partner than the UK for financing India's economic development.

BUILDING BREADTH AS WELL AS DEPTH

While boosting bilateral trade, investments and capital flows will provide the necessary depth for the India–UK partnership, we should also build some breadth. Take for example, financial technology, where London has a world-leading cluster of innovative companies; or retail and consumer sectors where we have similarly world-class merchandising and supply chain capabilities; and not forgetting our iconic creative industries; or the strengths of our defence sector too.

Fintech is a new string to the City of London's bow and provides strong alignment with India's financial inclusion agenda. India's 'Pradhan Mantri Jan-Dhan Yojana' (PMJDY), formally launched in August 2014 has led to the opening of 255 million bank accounts to ensure more comprehensive access to affordable financial services. Combined with Aadhaar (the national unique identity card scheme) and a database of mobile numbers, it provides the much-lauded 'JAM' (Jan-Dhan-Aadhaar-Mobile) trinity—which enables direct benefit transfers and eliminates leakages. The demonetisation programme has added a fourth dimension to the creation of a cashless society—allowing the previously unbanked to leapfrog into the digital economy—providing the UK's fintech sector with an unparalleled market opportunity.

Similarly, India's renewed burst of reform has finally permitted 'majority investment' in multi-brand retailing which is a brave political decision that has started to reshape an archaic retail sector. Companies such as Tesco already source over USD 500 million of goods from India, supporting competitive prices to the UK consumers. They now have the prospect of selling directly, and competitively, to Indian consumers and, in the process, transform the country's notoriously inefficient supply chains.

Hand in hand with mass consumerism of the retail sector are India's vibrant cultural industries spanning Bollywood, literature and cricket. The UK and India enjoy the rare accomplishment of genuine innovation through collaboration in the creative sector. Consider, for example, the role of British publishers in bringing to the world the award-winning works of authors such as Vikram Seth and Arundhati Roy.

Despite Britain's disappointment over the award of a multibillion Indian jet-fighter contract to a rival consortium, defence remains a 'hard' and historic area of immense bilateral collaboration. India's defence budget, already at over USD 50 billion, is one of the fastest growing in the world. With foreign suppliers required to plough back at least 30 per cent of the contract value into India as offsets, there is fertile ground for more India–UK defence partnerships—particularly those which provide genuine technology transfer, supporting Modi's 'Make in India' programme.

UNLEASHING THE MODI MAGIC

Meanwhile, Prime Minister Modi is entering a new, more intense period of his premiership. It is a game of two halves: Where the second phase of his parliamentary term should see the economic reform agenda shift gears.

I was present in India on 8 November 2016 when Modi announced his bold demonetisation initiative. Having accompanied Prime Minister Theresa May to India immediately before this, and coupled with Donald Trump's unexpected election victory immediately afterwards, it made for a highly memorable week.

I have also seen Modi up close as chief minister of Gujarat and negotiated the terms of significant corporate investments into the state, in fierce competition with other locations. The comparison was highly instructive.

Unlike any in his peer group, Chief Minister Modi, was more akin to a chief executive. He was in total command, leading from the front and was supported by an executive team of highly able and motivated administrators. The strategic vision was backed by a slick execution capability.

In comparison, Modi the Prime Minister has always felt shackled by bureaucratic inertia and a political straightjacket. With the demonetisation move we have finally seen signs that the original, undiluted Modi is back. However, the central execution capability in Delhi still needs work to match the dynamism of his previous machinery in Gujarat.

Before Modi was selected as the BJP's prime ministerial candidate, I had the pleasure of visiting him in Gujarat, in June 2013, together with my friend and now fellow peer in the House of Lords, Jim O'Neill—former Chief Economist of Goldman Sachs—who is famous for coining the BRIC acronym. We went on a forty-eight-hour trip to Ahmedabad to discuss with Modi how to achieve India's full economic potential. We elaborated on ten policy recommendations with 'governance' at the top of the list acting as the enabler for everything else. During the Vibrant Gujarat Lecture that marked our trip, Modi spoke for the first time openly about some of his own signature policy themes and also emphasised the journey from 'Minimum Government to Maximum Governance'.

It is clear that Modi has not lost sight of that journey and, when we look back, the demonetisation initiative may prove to be a turning point for both Modi and India.

CREATING NEW SPARKS

In conclusion, the opportunity set in India remains large and significant and the UK's aspiration for building shared prosperity is not just undimmed but positively galvanised by the compulsions of Brexit. Yet, the promise of India is not new, nor for the faint hearted. The erratic policymaking of the type that snowballed into a wall of critical commentary following the retroactive tax ruling on Vodafone was proof that India rarely moves in a straight line. Indian politics sometimes resembles Bollywood: Plenty of drama, intrigue and emotions before reaching a happy ending. But, aspiration always wins the day.

A respected Indian businessman described the India–UK relationship to me as being like a long married couple. We are so familiar with each other that it is easy to take each other for granted and sometimes we need to find a new spark to revive our relationship. I certainly hope we can encourage those new sparks and unlock the full potential of the India–UK partnership.

Lord Gadhia is a British Indian investment banker and businessman.

Laying the Groundwork for an India–UK Trade Deal

Hon Barry Gardiner MP

I had taken a delegation of Members of Parliament out to Gujarat in the aftermath of the 2001 earthquake. We were astonished by the force with which it had destroyed so much of the ancient city of Bhuj and we came with a cheque of £1 million for the reconstruction work to present to the new chief minister—a young political firebrand called Narendra Modi. I'd had the pleasure of meeting him a couple of years earlier before he had been elected and had shown him around 10 Downing Street. We had long discussions about election tactics over tea on the terrace of the House of Commons. And now here I was, getting out of an old Hindustan Ambassador car in a small village in the middle of Kutch when I realised just how inextricably linked our two countries were. Five feet away from me was a tall Indian gentleman aged about thirty. 'Hello Mr Gardiner! What are you doing here? You're my MP.'

My parliamentary constituency of Brent North was 4,000 miles away and I, a relatively new MP, could not step out into a village in India without being recognised by a constituent. Certainly Brent is one of the most diverse and multicultural communities anywhere on the planet and many of my constituents had come after a family journey that had taken them from

Gujarat to East Africa and finally to London to live beside the world-famous Wembley Stadium where, fourteen years later, Narendra Modi would address thousands of my constituents and others on his visit to the UK following his successful election as prime minister of India.

This is how trade links are made—friendships and family ties that create the bedrock of trust upon which all the best business deals and trade agreements are based—trade treaties that work to the benefit of both countries and raise living standards and create jobs that work to everyone's benefit. In 1999 I established Labour Friends of India and it is little surprise then that when I was a minister in the Department of Trade and Industry a decade ago, the first trade delegation I led was to New Delhi.

Since then I have met many, many wonderful people who share the same interests as I in advancing the long-standing trading relationship between India and the UK. Now in my capacity as the shadow secretary of state for international trade, I look forward to helping to forge new bonds between our great nations that will elevate standards, protections and incomes for all of our citizens.

The UK and India share a unique history with trade relations going back many hundreds of years. Indeed, British traders have traversed the Silk Road and transited the maritime spice trade routes for centuries. In the last twelve years that relationship has once again come under the spotlight, first with Tony Blair and the Delhi Declaration in 2005 and subsequently through the overtures of David Cameron and Theresa May. Today, I believe it is a relationship that will have much greater strategic as well as economic significance as India responds to the regional challenge of the rise of China and resurgence of Russia. India has to chart her relationships with her northern neighbours all the while setting out and her own need to establish herself as an equal global superpower. Britain can be helpful in enabling India to do that, whilst in the United Kingdom we seek to chart our own new path in the wake of the referendum vote to withdraw from the European Union.

The special relationship between our two countries extends to far more than just trade, however, it is trade that inherently binds us and that will ultimately define what our future relationship might look like. India won her independence from the United Kingdom in 1947 and since then has become one of the world's most powerful economies and one of the most attractive export markets with a population of some 1.25 billion people. Economic reforms, technological innovation and widespread social reforms have resulted in ever-increasing numbers in education and this has been the trigger for a rapid rise in GDP and household incomes. India's efforts to identify her core competencies and to invest heavily in talent development are beginning to bear fruit and the world recognises India's emerging strength as a technical and innovative powerhouse. This upward trend only continues to further the appeal of investing in India for overseas businesses.

The eyes of the world are closely fixed on India and the place that the country will take on the world stage and her emerging dominance in next-generation technology industries. India has challenged the conventional world view on emerging market economies and has taken a strong lead in the implementation of green technologies including the International Solar Alliance and a commitment to the provision of clean affordable energy for all its people. India has positioned itself as a global voice on climate action. The world gasped at the extraordinary turnaround India made as it cancelled its projected ultra-mega coal projects because of the rapid decline in the cost of solar power and other renewables. This has enabled India to be at the forefront, confirming her strong commitment to the global climate agreement. It is the old powerhouse economies of the developed world that are now being left behind and we would do well to pay attention.

India and the UK's special relationship is augmented by our respective memberships of the Commonwealth and the long rich cultural history which has seen many British business customs and legal traditions adopted in India as well as many Indian customs and traditions incorporated here in the UK.

It is this shared history and mutual Commonwealth membership that were used by many of those who campaigned for us to leave the European Union. Before the referendum vote they proclaimed a special message to the Indian diaspora that an end to free movement of people in the EU would be used to open up the UK to greater immigration from the Commonwealth. Strangely that friendly rhetoric has now faded away as the Brexit secretary now promises that migration will be reduced to tens of thousands. But one thing is sure: Now that Britain is leaving the EU, there must be a renewed focus on our trade relationship with India. Nostalgia and history alone do not constitute a sufficient basis for a modern trade relationship between our nations and both countries now need to take a hard look at the benefits and potential downsides of a bilateral free trade agreement.

The UK needs to set out what opportunities it has identified alongside India to grow and nurture a collaborative future industry. We need to recognise that our historic trading relationships have been the result of successful relationship-building between our peoples and the capacity to move goods and to offer services across our borders. But substantial barriers still remain.

The UK government has made a series of overtures to India in the wake of the European Referendum result here. As it seeks to pull away from the largest free trade area in the world, it has sought to build and cement relations with non-EU trading partners in a bid to mitigate the potential drop in exports and the corresponding damage to its balance of payments as a result of the fallout from Brexit. A number of ministerial visits and delegations from the UK to India culminated with the prime minister and the international trade secretary visiting India at the end of 2016 to promote trade between the world's oldest democracy and the world's largest democracy. They were right to go. But they should have sorted out beforehand what it was that they had to offer that India would most value.

India made it clear that it was not happy with the Conservative government's approach to migration and the Prime Minister's own track record in the Home Office where she abandoned the post-study work visa programme and Tier 4 visas. This has caused serious damage to our relationship. More than this, as one of the UK's strongest foreign direct investors, India had seen the UK as a safe conduit for Indian companies to enter the European market. Unsurprising then that long before the referendum, Prime Minister Modi had expressed his concern about the problems a 'Leave vote' would cause for Indian companies operating in Britain.

It is no longer possible for the UK ministers to appeal to a shared history or common social and cultural institutions and think these can be a substitute for a clear economic offer in a trade deal that represents a win-win for both sides. It has been 416 years since the East India Company's charter was signed in 1601. And British ministers need to realise that it cuts no ice today. In a globalised world, the dynamic of future trading relationships will inevitably pivot around deeper strategic alliances and the movement of people that commerce and trade has always involved.

The basis for securing preferential future trade terms with India begins in that recognition of essential equality. Indeed, it begins in recognising that India is now an emerging global superpower whose primary interests are regional in Southeast Asia and who needs a deal with the UK less than we need one with her.

The UK has been a leader in global trade punching above its weight for three centuries. Our success has been based not only upon military might; it has sprung from world-leading universities and a strong science base; it has been nurtured by embedded legal institutions which guarantee swift and impartial redress in commercial contract disputes, and it has blossomed through a period of manufacturing innovation that gave the world the first industrial revolution. But our exports now are predominantly service-based and this changes the dynamic of trade, particularly with countries such as India. India wants access to our educational institutions and it has much to gain from our professional services, but it has a political imperative to protect its agricultural base and dare not choke off its emerging middle class by opening up its financial services and retail sectors in the way the UK would like.

India was keen to secure a trade and investment agreement with the EU, officially known as the Broad-based Trade and Investment Agreement (BTIA). Negotiations began in June 2007 but ultimately collapsed in 2013 following twelve rounds of formal talks. If the UK is to succeed where Europe failed, the new Department for International Trade must study carefully why the terms on offer from the EU were insufficient to tempt India into an agreement. It must also swiftly develop a realistic sense of its own importance. The UK is India's eighteenth-largest trading partner. The EU collectively was its first. India's largest single trading partner is China and a number of other Middle Eastern and Asian countries make the list ahead of the United Kingdom.

Trade negotiations require compromise. The extent to which the government is willing to consider compromises with respect to any future trade deal with India, with simultaneous talks with the EU, will profoundly influence how willing the rest of the world will be to engage in their own talks with us and what role we will play in wider international affairs. India will want to see a substantive offer from the UK that is worth its lowering tariffs and other barriers to its markets. It is clear what India wants. What is not clear is whether this UK government is prepared to liberalise the movement of people in the way that India would like.

India is, understandably, keen to develop its own market economy and domestic skill sets rather than to rely on knowledge, goods and services imported from overseas. Modi's government wants to facilitate Indian citizens moving freely to provide services—particularly in the IT sector, building on Mode 4 of the WTO's General Agreement on Trade in Services. This agenda has run counter to the UK's own agenda which has seemingly been about reducing migrant numbers and ensuring the preservation of Geographical Indications for key exports like Scotch whisky.

During the many years of negotiations, some progress was made with respect to areas such as rice, sugar, textiles and pharmaceuticals, and to some extent the wine sector but stumbled over access to India's highly regulated professional services, financial services and government procurement markets. The UK is a service-led economy with professional services and financial services being our biggest export. As former British ambassador to Korea, Sir Thomas Harris said at a recent summit in London: 'For the life of me, I cannot see why the Indians would be prepared to offer concessions in services in bilateral talks which they were not prepared to offer in return for access to the EU as a whole.'

India is the third-largest destination in value terms for foreign direct investment from the UK. But the UK is also the third-largest destination for FDI from India. The two-way flow of investment and capital is intrinsic to our capacity to augment and progress our trade relationships but we have to be willing to recognise how much of this has been predicated on our capacity to attract and retain talent from India as well as the significant contribution that British Indian entrepreneurs and investors have made to developing our own market and in creating businesses that drive that trade between our two nations. So many British SMEs are owned or managed by people who came to the UK to seek a better life for themselves and their families—many of these will grow to become the international corporations of our future and we recognise the need to ensure that our trade policy nurtures and grows these businesses ensuring that they have maximum support to export and invest here and overseas. We need to let these business owners know that we value their contribution and welcome their growth.

India will also be wary of British prime ministers who seek to celebrate the unique relationship between the UK and India whenever they visit, only to pour scorn on aid programmes and development support to India when they are back home. Of course, India is one of the world's fastest-developing economies. But because of her vast size and population, it is no secret that the benefits of this growth have not yet reached all corners of society. The UK should see overseas aid as an investment in the future potential of a market and it shouldn't be used as a stick to bash trading partners and strategic allies with. The value of the UK aid-spending in India is that it has ensured that we are able to work with our partners to develop their markets, business and enterprise, to boost labour standards and rights, and ultimately, to boost the incomes of the poorest, which, in the long term, boosts demand for British goods and services.

This is why in September 2016, at the Labour Party Conference, I announced the Just Trading Initiative, which will see like-minded politicians from across the globe coming together to develop a progressive trade agenda that seeks to promote such rights and standards, alongside protections for the environment and the rights of governments to legislate in the public interest. Twentieth-century world views and approaches to international affairs no longer have a place in an interconnected, globalised economy—we have to look at how we are able to work with our partners towards shared objectives that benefit all of our citizens and not just a few high net worth individuals or multinational corporations. That is why Labour will promote small and medium-sized enterprises as the fundamental drivers of future economic growth and international trade as we recognise that a future international trade agenda fit for purpose must promote collaborative working between SMEs and MNCs alike, innovators and inventors across borders in order to grow next-generation industries together.

But we cannot support the growth and expansion of any businesses, small or large, until it is clear who our trading partners will be and under what restrictions such trade might take place. Businesses are currently paralysed with uncertainty and are being prevented from pursuing investment. Business leaders are repeatedly calling for the government to set out what their priorities are for Britain's future trading agenda. If the UK cannot find the ground upon which to advance a trade agreement with India, then the British people may well feel that they have been lied to by those who promised that we would secure a flurry of trade deals in quick succession with Commonwealth partners and key international allies.

We have reached a critical juncture in our respective histories, not just with respect to our own relations but also with respect to our relationships with other countries. Here in Britain, we are aware of the impact of our declining political focus on engagement with India and politicians from all parties are working hard to repair these relationships. The Labour Party knows that support of no community can be taken for granted and we must work to maintain the trust and affection of the NRI community here in the UK as the oldest and truest friends of India.

With this in mind, it is time for British politicians from all parties to face reality and to take off the rose-tinted glasses and start looking to Britain's future relationships and not our past. We must strategically plan not only our own place in the world but also what place our friends and allies will have and how we can work together to ensure that we share the skills, talent and successes to build commercial ties and trading agreements that can fulfil the aspirations of all our people.

Barry Gardiner is the Shadow Secretary of State for International Trade.

Inspiring Indian Students to Join the UK Universities: Key to Long-term Relationship

Lord Karan Bilimoria

I came to the UK as a student in the early 1980s because of the world-class education that was on offer here. I am the third generation of my family, on both sides, to be educated here in the UK, but when I first arrived Britain was known as the sick man of Europe—a country that had lost an empire and found no real purpose, a has-been. The City of London was a closed shop; prejudice was rife. In fact, I was told by my family and friends in India, 'If you decide to work in Britain after your studies you will not get to the top, you will not be allowed to. There will be a glass ceiling for you as a foreigner.' Three decades ago, they were absolutely right.

Britain has transformed in front of my eyes over the past thirty years, from the sick man of Europe into the envy of Europe. The glass ceiling has been shattered. The country is truly aspirational and meritocratic—a place where anyone can get as far as their aspirations, talent and hard work will let them, regardless of race, religion or background. London today is one of the most cosmopolitan cities in the world and Britain is respected as a global power around the world.

The UK has so much to offer international students: A dynamic country that is cosmopolitan yet steeped in history, proud of its heritage and outward-facing. That is why thousands of ambitious, gifted and enterprising young Indians come to our shores every year to learn at some of the best institutions in the world. The opportunity to study here was life-changing for me. It was the foundation on which I built my business, Cobra Beer, and a formative period during which I decided to become an entrepreneur who is proud to call the UK home over thirty years later.

The UK's universities are the jewel in the national crown. Alongside those of the United States of America, the UK's universities are the best in the world. A Britain without its universities is almost incomprehensible; they have contributed so much to this enterprising nation, and contribute more every year. Education does not just hold the keys to a student's future but also to a closer relationship between the UK and India. At a time of unquantifiable change, the UK and India ought to look to each other as guarantors of their informed, enlightened futures.

THE BREXIT FACTOR: AN OPPORTUNITY FOR THE UK–INDIA HIGHER EDUCATION COLLABORATION

Just like every other major part of British economy and society, the nation's higher education system must wait with bated breath until it finds out exactly how it will be affected by the UK's decision to leave the European Union.

It is likely that funding programmes will take a massive blow. Take the University of Cambridge, for example: It was the largest recipient of €80 billion that was made available through the EU-backed Horizon 2020 initiative. It is unknown whether the funding will continue.

Similar uncertainty looms over the heads of teaching staff from across the EU. Some 16.5 per cent of staff at the University of Cambridge is European Economic Area (EEA) nationals. When it comes to MPhils, that figure is 21 per cent; for PhD students, it is 27 per cent.

International students at the undergraduate and postgraduate levels contribute, directly and indirectly, £25 billion to the UK economy and support 137,000 full time-equivalent jobs across the country. Higher education is one of the UK's most valuable exports. But it's about more than just economics.

Foreign students enrich the experience of our domestic students and higher education is one of the UK's most potent sources of soft power. Our international scholars go on to become world leaders, with an estimated one in ten global heads of state educated in the UK, and I speak from experience when I say that overseas students form generations-long links with domestic students and the nation itself.

Students from overseas have helped the UK become a pioneer in a range of fields, including science and technology. For example, Sir Venki Ramakrishnan, Nobel Laureate and fellow of Trinity College, Cambridge, is the first Indian ever to become president of the Royal Society, a position held by many scientific greats including Sir Isaac Newton.

The UK universities already attract Indian students in huge numbers—only China sends more—but Britain cannot be complacent. In the words of the former UK Prime Minister David Cameron, Britain is engaged in a 'global race'. The UK is competing with every other country in the world and the UK's 400-year-old historical ties are not enough. Britain needs to properly showcase the entrepreneurial and dynamic place it is, in order to inspire students from the world's largest democracy.

The UK government's muddled attitude towards overseas students has led to the number of new non-EU students arriving in the UK decrease by 2 per cent in 2015, whilst the number of Indian students coming to the UK has halved in the past five years. Meanwhile, the USA increased its overall numbers by 9 per cent including an almost 25 per cent increase in students from India.

Claims that the number of international students ought to fall because it reflects the will of the British people, as expressed in the EU referendum, to see real controls on immigration and a tightening of the UK borders are simply untrue. According to Universities UK, almost 80 per cent of the British population wants international students to stay on and work in the UK after they finish their studies.

The same research found that just 22 per cent of British people think that international students should be classed as 'immigrants'. In many countries—including our competitors—international students are classified differently, often as 'temporary migrants'. Theresa May, who failed to resolve this issue during her tenure as home secretary, would not be risking popularity in making the change; these reforms might actually be received favourably.

The UK, an island nation and only 1 per cent of the world's population, is in spite of that the sixth-largest economy in the world. This is in many ways thanks to immigration, which has brought so much value to our country. India plays no small role in that. There are almost one and half million Indians living in our country and they are among the most successful and valuable immigrant populations we have in the UK.

They have reached the top in almost every imaginable field; be it in sport and entertainment, in architecture, design and the creative industries, in science and technology, in innovation and research, in business and in politics, Indians have given us reasons to celebrate the diversity of our great nation every step of the way.

Now, with Brexit, it is imperative that the government seeks to use this chance instead to forge closer-than-ever ties with India. Yet, on a trip to India in November 2016, the UK Prime Minister, Theresa May, failed to do just that.

BREAKING GROUND WITH THE UK–INDIA BUSINESS COUNCIL

The UK prime minister's November 2016 delegation to India was littered with missed opportunities. On the eve of the trip it was announced that the minimum annual salary threshold for Tier 2 visas, used by Indian IT workers—one of India's most prominent exports and a vital catalyst for economic growth in the UK tech sector—would rise from £21,000 to £35,000. This simultaneously damaged our ability to attract global talent and made Indian IT exports to the UK less competitive, souring our relations with India.

Indian IT workers have enabled digital technology to become the UK's fastest-growing sector, significantly bolstering the development of the Silicon Roundabout. Silicon Valley has made the most of its Indian diaspora, with a large number of 'unicorns'—start-up companies valued at over USD 1 billion—developed by Indians. If the UK wants to continue as the 'unicorn' capital of Europe, it needs to follow the US's example.

In Theresa May's opening speech in India, alongside Narendra Modi at the Tech Summit, she did not mention universities or Indian students at all.

Neither did she meet with any of the thirty-five university leaders from the higher education sector from the UK who were accompanying the Universities Minister Jo Johnson in India at the time. On the other hand, her Indian counterpart, Prime Minister Narendra Modi, stressed that 'education is vital for our students…therefore we must encourage greater mobility and participation of young people in education and research opportunities.' Prime Minister Modi's statement hinted at one of the UK government's fatal misunderstandings: Trade deals are about more than just tariffs, they are about relationships and the movement of people. With the Secretary of State for International Trade Liam Fox, boasting about the UK's ability to conduct trade deals with India, while offering little in return, there is little wonder that the UK–India relationship is now viewed as purely transactional for many in India.

When questioned by the BBC on whether India's long-standing relationship with the UK would lead to an accelerated trade deal between the two countries, Nirmala Sitharaman, India's minister of state for commerce and industry, stated: 'Well, I thought so and most of us in India thought so, but we aren't being treated as old friends any longer. It's a tight professional engagement.'

The allegiance between the UK and India is so much more than a mere professional engagement. India and the UK trade on common principles; both embrace the freedom of speech, have a free and vibrant press, uphold the rule of law, respect open and liberal democracy and nurture economic growth.

On the strength of these common principles, I founded the UK–India Business Council and was its founding chairman in 2007. This brought together both the private sector and the public sector supported by UK Trade and Investment (UKTI) to promote trade, business and investment in both directions between the UK and India.

This was after the Bharatiya Janata Party (BJP) lost power in India in 2004. Over the course of their time in power, from 1999-2004, the BJP government had brought the economy its biggest boom in over a decade. However, they were voted out of government. I saw the challenges India faced, as a developing nation; India is the most diverse country in the world in every way—in terrain, in race, in religion—and despite the BJP's success, its economic growth was not seen to be inclusive enough. It needed job-creating economic growth, infrastructure improvements and greater clean energy supplies throughout the cities and the rural areas too. Here, there was a chance for the UK and India to bring together their combined resources and collaborate to share trading opportunities.

Today, some of Prime Minister Theresa May's ministers stand out because they recognise the importance of Britain's ties with India: As part of the Prime Minister's first foreign trade delegation, in India, Jo Johnson—the minister for universities, science, research and innovation—highlighted the power of collaboration between the UK and India.

Jo Johnson cited impact ratings from collaborative research conducted by researchers from the University of Birmingham and Panjab University. In only one year, since we signed our memorandum of understanding, we have already conducted ground-breaking research together in areas such as cancer therapies, and this builds on a long-lasting connection, with many of the Indian population in Birmingham and the West Midlands being from the Punjab region. The two groups of researchers are doing vital work at a time when manufacturing is becoming more advanced and cybersecurity is increasingly more vital to the infrastructure on which we rely.

However, the two universities working together can achieve an impact rating of 5.64 with their joint research papers, more than three times the score that either university achieves individually (1.37 for Panjab University, 1.87 for the University of Birmingham), and virtually identical to the score achieved when the University of Birmingham conducts research jointly with Harvard University. The power of collaboration is brilliant and highly dependable and it can work on a greater scale.

Indian Prime Minister Narendra Modi has a number of initiatives in place to modernise the economy and attract inward investment, such as Smart Cities and Make in India—with which he has set a target to increase the manufacturing sector's share of GDP from 16 to 25 per cent. India can be a vital partner for the UK as we tackle our own modern challenges and seek to rebalance our economy and improve our economic productivity.

Targets, Tier 2s and Bottom Lines: Back to the Visa Question

Britain invests more in India than any other G20 country, and India invests more in Britain than in all other EU countries combined. It is a solid foundation on which to build stronger trading ties, but an overhaul of visa and work permit policy in the UK is required.

An Indian fast-track visa system, similar to the technology enterprise visa scheme, would send a clear message to India that we are open for business. For Indian nationals who frequently come to the UK, the entry process will become significantly easier, with fewer forms to fill out, access to the EU/EEA passport control and swifter passage through our airports.

China too is seen as a vital partner for the UK. During the Chinese President Xi Jinping's 2015 visit to Britain, then Prime Minister David Cameron launched the two-year multiple-entry visa scheme for Chinese tourists, which could be purchased for the discounted cost of £85 rather than £330. Bearing in mind the historic significance of the UK's ties with India, sharing the scheme with Indian visitors makes a great deal of sense. It has support from many, including the UK businesses that would stand to gain a great deal from Indian business visitors, as well as from a boost in tourism from India—a vast nation of over a billion people. Tourism in the UK has been the fastest-growing sector in employment terms, but we will fall far short of a projected twofold increase in the value of the tourism industry by 2025 if we cannot encourage access for our largest markets.

The Home Office's claim that 90,000 international students a year overstay, one of the long-standing arguments for counting students in the net migration target, has now been thoroughly debunked. The International Passenger Survey (IPS), used to calculate net migration, is considered unreliable and it is increasingly clear that the vast majority of international students come to the UK, study for a period and return home. Data derived from exit checks implemented at the UK borders suggest that only 1,500 students (around 1 per cent) do not leave each year.

In 1998, shortly after he came to power, Prime Minister Tony Blair abolished exit checks at our borders, but we need to bring back comprehensive entry and exit checks for everyone coming into and out of the UK so that we know exactly who has been coming into our country. Otherwise, the gap in perception will only persist. The government has a target to reduce net migration to the tens of thousands from the current 335,000, yet ministers continue to categorise international students as immigrants. This sends out a catastrophically bad signal to prospective students, including those from India.

Globally, the number of university students looking to study abroad is expected to grow from 4.1 million in 2010 to 8 million globally by 2025. And the UK, with 10 per cent, currently has the second-highest share of international students globally, after the United States (at 19 per cent). The UK is therefore in a prime position to capitalise on this projected growth, but we need the government to act, and act quickly.

Canada aims to double its numbers by 2020, while Australia wants to increase international students to 720,000 by 2025. The former Australian Education Minister Christopher Pyne went so far as to thank Britain for its immigration policies because they had driven so many students to Australia's universities!

The two-year post-study work visa, which I fought hard to introduce in 2007, was scrapped in 2012. It allowed foreign students to implement their much-needed skills and help boost our economy, as well as gain work experience and further build generational bridges with our country. It should be re-implemented without delay.

We need to implement a comprehensive strategy to increase the number of international students into the UK in line with our competitors. We need to send the message to the rest of the world that the UK is the top destination in the world for the brightest and the best.

CONCLUSION

In a year of rhetoric which pivoted around the EU referendum, the importance of the UK's higher education sector has been vastly overlooked. The message sent across the world by British politicians, playing to the UKIP gallery, has come at a great cost. The outcome of this astonishing vote has not just affected our relationships with generations of leaders in the business sector and the public eye around the world; it has had an immediate impact on the higher education sector, with applications from EU students to British universities falling, despite an overall rise in university applications globally.

The UK needs to establish itself once more as an outward-facing nation with the right environment for international talent to thrive. At present, the world is beginning to see us as inward-looking, insular and increasingly intolerant. That is not the Britain I know and love.

Britain has always been a country with integrity. The word integrity comes from the Latin word 'integritas', which means wholeness. You cannot practice integrity if you are fragmented. You can practice integrity only if you are whole and complete. Britain needs to retain its wholeness and completeness so that we can always practice integrity.

Lord Bilimoria CBE is Founder-Chairman of Cobra Beer and President of the UK Council for International Student Affairs.

BUSINESS VOICES

Maintaining Momentum in a New Era of Economic Cooperation

Chandrajit Banerjee

Historically linked together for centuries, India and the United Kingdom share a commitment to democracy, peace and stability as also institutional, educational and legal affinities that underpin the vibrant and dynamic bilateral relationship today. As India embarks on a reinvigorated growth path and the UK prepares for a historic detachment from the EU, these shared foundations establish a new era of economic cooperation that extends into multiple domains in alignment with the rapid changes taking place in the world today.

The visit of Hon'ble Prime Minister Narendra Modi to the UK in November 2015 is considered a milestone in the overall relationship, identifying new areas of cooperation in a vision statement, including a renewed focus on investments, commercial cooperation, infrastructure, energy and climate change among others.

The India visit of Theresa May, prime minister of the UK, as her first bilateral visit outside the European continent in November 2016, further deepened and strengthened this journey. The process has been carried forward through frequent visits of ministers, officials and businesses in both directions, and promises to elevate the engagement between the world's largest democracy and its oldest.

Given the evolving dynamic scenario of India's growth and the new situation arising in the UK, the overall ecosystem for the India–UK relationship is shifting. The two countries must be prepared to consider fundamental re-engineering of their economic relations. This must include exploring new frontiers of cooperation across areas such as advanced technology, R&D, higher education and skill development, urban growth, and sectors of manufacturing, infrastructure and services; recalibration of enabling policies including labour mobility and skilling initiatives; and joint consultations on our framework economic cooperation agreements. There is need to go beyond the conventional areas of cooperation to leverage new developments in the emerging knowledge economy and accentuate cooperation to harness the gains from India's development journey.

THE NEW INDIA

In a period of slowing global growth, India stands out as an oasis, experiencing 7.6 per cent GDP growth in the financial year 2015-16, and widely expected to maintain a high-growth path for some time to come. India is in a sweet spot with its macroeconomic fundamentals including inflation, fiscal deficit and current account at prudent levels, thanks to astute management in the recent past. Demographic factors such as a growing workforce and declining age-dependency ratios accompanied by rising education and human development levels contribute to a rapidly-expanding domestic market that is emerging as one of the largest consumer destinations in the world. The bold step of replacing high-value currency notes with new currency notes in late 2016 was a body-blow for corruption, and was widely welcomed by ordinary citizens.

India has set in motion a range of large-scale campaigns designed to boost the pace of poverty alleviation and growth, as also address gaps in infrastructure and the social sector. The Jan-Dhan Yojana is the largest financial inclusion programme in the world and has succeeded in opening almost 260 million no-frills bank accounts. Over 1 billion unique identity cards, named the Aadhaar Card, have been issued to citizens, while a similar number of mobile phones offers the extraordinary opportunity to link social security, digital technology and financial access.

The Make in India mission aims to greatly expand manufacturing and job creation through a focus on industrial corridors and parks. The mission includes a range of strategic vectors designed to ramp up the pace of manufacturing growth and create 100 million new jobs. The strategies are aimed at creating new infrastructure and connectivity, designing a facilitative investment climate, attracting foreign direct investments (FDI), strengthening the intellectual property rights regime, developing necessary skill capabilities and addressing twenty-five key sectors. These sectors have been especially identified for promotional policies and are emerging as lead sectors for the manufacturing endeavour.

Efforts to improve the ease of doing business have been undertaken in a focused manner with the cooperation of India's state governments for improving the investment climate. The regulatory environment for FDI has been consistently eased, opening new sectors for participation of overseas investors such as defence manufacturing, real estate, insurance, medical devices, aviation and railway production, among others.

In infrastructure, a range of new initiatives has led to an explosion in roads and highways construction, power and renewable energy capacities and airport connectivity. The Smart Cities Mission is scripting a new urbanisation story that will converge physical and digital infrastructures. Equally, the Digital India campaign is driving digital access, electronics manufacturing and e-governance in a multipronged endeavour with remarkable success. Skill India has already brought new capabilities to over 10 million youth from government initiatives, and private sector training is adding to this effort.

Each of these areas offers renewed opportunities for future collaboration between India and the UK.

BILATERAL ECONOMIC RELATIONS

India and the UK have established a strong dialogue mechanism that includes government-to-government interaction supported by greater interaction between their private sectors. The India–UK Economic and Financial Dialogue, initiated in 2005, is a platform to discuss common responses to global economic challenges, macroeconomic environment, infrastructure finance and financial services. A key outcome from its most recent meeting in January 2016 was collaboration on the emerging sectors of the Indian economy including smart cities, renewable energy and railways. Financial technology, or fintech, was especially identified to enhance India's financial inclusion outreach.

The India–UK Joint Economic and Trade Committee (JETCO) brings in the private-sector component with businesses of both countries actively participating in the dialogue with the two economic and trade ministers. The tenth meeting of JETCO, held in London in January 2015, set up working groups to focus on education and skill development, smart cities, technological collaboration, advanced manufacturing and engineering. These sectors align with India's developmental needs, the UK's economic strengths and the emerging global knowledge economy.

The India–UK CEO Forum, another high-level platform for industry, brings business leaders together to discuss challenges and opportunities in the business relationship. Their six identified work streams—(1) Smart cities and the digital economy, (2) Healthcare and hygiene, (3) Education, (4) Manufacturing, defence and security, (5) Financial and professional services and (6) Bilateral ease of doing business—have significant activity underway along with concrete recommendations to enhance the India–UK partnership.

Theresa May's visit to India in November 2016 added further impetus to the economic partnership. Addressing the India–UK CII-DST TECH Summit organised by CII and the Department of Science and Technology as part of CII's series of technology summits, the Prime Minister stated that Indian business visitors would now be eligible for the Registered Traveller scheme of the UK which is aimed at a facilitative visa regime. She stressed that with Brexit, the UK would forge a new global outlook and her visit to India, her first bilateral visit outside Europe as prime minister and her first trade mission, was aimed at greater trade and investment and fewer trade barriers.

With a large trade delegation accompanying her, the stress was on economic engagement and addressing barriers to trade. Two agreements were signed on ease of doing business and intellectual property rights. During the India–UK CEO Forum held in conjunction with the visit, the two sides agreed to set up an advanced material and manufacturing technology centre in India.

TRADE

Overall trade in goods and services grew strongly between 2010 and 2013, going up from £16.7 billion to £20.6 billion, with growth in both directions. However, trade has been on a downward slope since 2013. This could be attributed to subdued global economic and trade conditions.

While trade in services has been fairly stable, trade in goods has been experiencing a steeper decline. It is worth noting that total trade has slipped from £20.6 billion in 2013 to £16.3 billion in 2015—a decline of over 20 per cent in two years. Total trade in 2015, after some fluctuations, was back at roundabout 2010 levels, suggesting a plateau in growth.

INVESTMENTS

Bilateral investments are the exciting growth narrative in economic engagement. The UK is the third-largest investor in India and the largest among the G20 countries and from Europe. It is more interesting that India has emerged as the third-largest investor in the UK. In 2015, Indian investments rose by a whopping 65 per cent, affirming the interest of Indian companies in doing business with the UK.

According to the latest edition of 'India Meets Britain', a report by Grant Thornton in collaboration with CII on the fastest-growing Indian companies in the UK, over 800 Indian companies operate in the UK and support 110,000 jobs. The fastest-growing of these companies, with growth rates of at least 10 per cent or higher, have a combined turnover of £26 billion. Their investment spans technology, telecom, pharmaceuticals and chemicals, financial services and other sectors. Nearly 40 per cent of Indian companies are concentrated in and around the London area, 34 per cent are spread in the south, 15 per cent in the north and 10 per cent in the Midlands.

Indian businesses view the UK as an attractive investment destination since it offers advanced engineering acumen, globalised and expert financial services sector, proximity to the larger EU market and access to technology and highly-regarded brands. Indians are also lured by the UK's advanced R&D and design expertise, increasingly competitive tax structure and facilitative business environment.

Similarly, a report by the Confederation of British Industry (CBI), supported by PricewaterhouseCoopers and the UK–India Business Council titled 'Sterling Assets: India', highlights the growing presence of the UK companies in India. It estimates that these companies employ about 691,000 people across the country and enjoy a revenue of more than USD 54 billion. In 2000-15, FDI from the UK came in at over USD 22 billion, flowing into sectors such as chemicals, pharmaceuticals, food processing and services.

Brexit and India

The UK's decision to exit from the EU is not expected to dent bilateral engagement to a significant extent, given the strong partnership that the two countries have built and their economic complementarities. India's economy is largely driven by domestic consumption rather than exports, and its exposure in terms of exports to the UK is relatively limited. While India may be impacted through second-round shocks emanating from a global financial system that remains fragile, its strong macroeconomic fundamentals, high foreign exchange reserves and lower integration with the world would help to maintain stability in the growth process, analysts believe.

CII is confident that Brexit offers positive opportunities for India and the UK to work together. Currently, India and the EU are negotiating a free trade agreement, a process that has been underway for nine years. After Brexit, India and the UK could work on a bilateral economic cooperation agreement that could be faster and may aid the process by bypassing some of the sticking points in the India–EU FTA.

Further, the UK could consider relaxing its investment regime as it relates to facilitating high-skilled professional labour mobility in order to facilitate higher fund flows from non-EU members, including India.

A CII's CEOs delegation to the UK in July 2016, just a week after the historic Brexit decision, was reassured by the statements of political leaders, businesspersons and academics that India would remain a priority for the UK economy. While there are real concerns and uncertainties that Indian businesses face and we must keep a close eye on unfolding developments and emerging policies, we must also take every opportunity to communicate our top priorities to the policymakers in the evolving business climate. We in the Indian industry feel that these concerns would be addressed going forward and the India–UK relationship would continue to strengthen.

CONTOURS OF FUTURE COOPERATION

Our future partnership derives from the strong existing foundation of cooperation, India's accelerated journey to development under the leadership of Prime Minister Modi, mutual interest of businesses on both sides and the overall evolution of the global knowledge economy where the UK assumes a prominent position. What can we do, as important stakeholders in this landscape to enhance the future of India–UK economic relationship? The road map for future cooperation is tied to emerging post-Brexit policies, a fresh perspective on economic partnership agreement and technology collaboration:

BRING IN POST-BREXIT CLARITY

The post-Brexit scenario in the UK remains inadequately clear for international businesses. While the negotiations commence and the direction of its future role in the EU is addressed, the UK must send out strong signals regarding the potential for Indian companies. The visit of the UK Prime Minister, Theresa May, to India in November 2016 was one such clear signal and sets a base for future engagement.

One area that needs to be taken up is the contribution of Indian companies in the UK in terms of job creation. As the third-largest foreign investor in the UK, Indian companies contribute to the UK economy and create many jobs. We need to resolutely dispel the perception that India, due to its competitive costs, is taking away jobs. Indian companies need to be reassured that the UK will continue to attract and allow the best of global talent for business.

In this context, it is important to continue to encourage the movement of Indians to the UK for all purposes, including tourism, higher education, work and business. Higher visa fees, stringent post-study work regulations and restrictive employment permits curtail the gains to the UK from operations and presence of Indian companies and workers.

Indian companies will derive comfort from clarity on emerging UK policies on single market access and passporting rights or the right of financial services companies with legal entity in the UK to operate across European markets. The UK must take care to avoid excessive restrictions on business operations from within its borders to the larger EU market.

CONSIDERING AN INDIA–UK TRADE/ECONOMIC COOPERATION AGREEMENT

India and the UK have the opportunity to commence on a bilateral trade agreement or comprehensive economic cooperation agreement. This should include trade in goods, trade in services, investments, mutual recognition of certifications and so on. Such a treaty would open up larger avenues for partnership.

A key aspect of such an agreement would be to negotiate good mobility for Indian companies operating in the UK. Visas, social security norms and short-term contract facilities should be offered for Indian companies. On the Indian side, it is necessary for India to provide greater access to the UK companies in areas such as higher education and professional services.

The UK companies should also be encouraged to work with Indian universities on R&D and innovation. It would be a huge advantage for India to build collaborations in design, particularly in skill development for the sector. The UK could consider partnering in a national design institute under India's 2007 Design Policy which aims at building a network of such institutes.

While formal decisions cannot be taken until the UK completes its exit process from the EU, an initialising discussion could at least bring forth key elements that would be crucial for such an agreement to materialise.

GOING HIGH-TECH TOGETHER

Today, India is progressing rapidly towards a knowledge-led, knowledge-driven economy. Our youth is increasingly internet-connected and tech-savvy. Combined with their innate sense of creativity and entrepreneurship, the young are leading the change to a new India. Frugal engineering, innovative thinking and tailored solutions are the hallmarks of the new knowledge economy in India.

India today has more than 1 billion phone connections and an urban teledensity of 148 per cent with a total of 350 million internet users. India's internet consumption is already more than that of the US, and the second largest in the world. By 2020, India is expected to have 730 million internet users, with total gross merchandise value of e-commerce increasing from just USD 2.9 billion in 2013 to over USD 100 billion by 2020.

The UK enjoys leadership strength in technology and innovation. It has much to offer to India, as also much to gain from partnering with it. The two countries would need to jointly address policy instruments in order to maximise the gains from their partnership.

The CII, in collaboration with Indian and UK governments, organised the first-ever India–UK Tech Summit in November 2016 in Delhi during the visit of Prime Minister May, where over 3,000 delegates came together to discuss and build technology-driven partnerships. This should not be a one-off effort—rather, the key to enhancing India–UK economic relations will be a sustained momentum in facilitating business ties and linkages.

To facilitate such ongoing engagement, we have also launched a virtual platform, India–UK Business Exchange, which works as a B2B matchmaking tool, enabling companies in India and the UK to find business venture partners, connect with them and discuss ideas.

PARTNERING ON SMART CITIES AND URBAN REGENERATION

India's Smart Cities Mission is meant to usher in a new era of urbanisation. The UK has committed to developing the smart cities of Pune, Amaravati and Indore. With these lighthouse cities, new areas of cooperation will be created in the overall trade and economic relationship.

The UK has expertise in infrastructure, smart transport solutions, professional services and e-governance. It is a global leader in design, spatial data analysis, modelling and visualisation. The UK firms supply a range of innovative, user-focused design systems to the world and can expand their presence in India's rapid urbanisation process.

A concerted effort to connect companies with opportunities in this sector could have wide-ranging and wide-scale implications for India–UK economic relations.

FINANCIAL SERVICES

The participation of the UK in India's rapidly-developing financial services sector can be beneficial for both sides. Fintech is emerging as the next big transformation for India as more than 220 million new households are brought into the umbrella of the Jan-Dhan Yojana. The Indian government targets leveraging the rapid spread of mobile telephones and the 1 billion unique identification cards or Aadhaar for direct benefits transfer.

A renewed push towards digital financial transactions following demonetisation plus new regulations has made this the robust start-up sector in India. The fintech software market is expected to double to over USD 2 billion by 2020. With smartphones and e-commerce, the sector could grow to a transaction value of USD 73 billion by that year, and even more with the effort to move towards a less-cash economy. With the UK's leadership in financial technology and international finance, the sector offers huge new opportunities for collaboration. India can also learn from the UK on how to develop an international finance hub.

Conclusion

The future of India–UK relations looks strong under the leadership of the two prime ministers and has acquired a positive glow of new opportunities. With each visit, the dimensions of cooperation enlarge and deepen, embracing more and more activities. Enterprises of both countries are keen to maintain the momentum and build closer economic synergies. This gains from the leading position of the UK in the evolving knowledge economy, as also from India's renewed growth vigour.

The future strategies can converge with India's development mission and the new synergies between the governments and businesses of the two sides would stand as a paradigm of partnership.

Chandrajit Banerjee is the Director-General of the Confederation of Indian Industry (CII).

Making India High Priority for
the UK Companies

RT HON PATRICIA HEWITT

As the UK's new Prime Minister, Theresa May chose India for her first bilateral visit outside Europe. The symbolism of the visit, in November 2016, was appreciated by India's political and business leaders who clearly welcomed her message that the Brexit referendum did not mean that Britain was turning inwards or protectionist, but instead rebalancing its relationships to give greater priority to the rest of the global economy in general and to India in particular. Whatever one's view of the referendum, there is no doubt that India—already one of the UK's most important global partners—is now an even higher priority for the British government.

At a time when global trade is—for the first time in decades—growing more slowly than the global economy, and in the week when the United States elected a president who campaigned on an overtly protectionist and anti-trade platform, it was good to hear PM May at the India–UK Tech Summit in Delhi unashamedly proclaiming the benefits of global trade. Her ambition, she said, is to make Britain the 'most committed and passionate advocate of free trade in the world'.[1]

I have no doubt that, as our prime minister said, trade between two countries benefits both of them. Consumers in Western and developing countries alike have enjoyed for many decades the cheaper consumer goods produced by supply chains that span the world. Low-income families in the UK, the US and elsewhere have particularly benefited from falling real prices in clothing, food, mobile phones, electronics and household goods.

But while trade benefits us all as consumers, its impact on people as producers may be highly disruptive. This is where the social and political problems lie. Workers at Tata Steel in Port Talbot fear for their jobs in the face of China's enormous steel plants. Indian farmers fear for their livelihoods if India opens up to Europe's food producers. In both cases, the argument is that free trade may not be fair trade: China's support for state-owned industries on the one hand, Europe's agricultural subsidies on the other. The protests of Indian farmers and the tragic suicides of some inhibited Indian governments in the WTO's Doha Round of negotiations. And today, the threats to steel workers' jobs in Europe and the US make a trade war with China all too possible.

In the early 2000s, as secretary of state for trade and industry, I feared a serious protectionist backlash as British banks started to move call centres from the UK to India. I argued very publicly that 'a job created in India does not mean a job lost in Britain'. I did my best to persuade people that, as India grew, millions of Indian families would escape from abject poverty— something we should all applaud. But I also argued that there was no contradiction between principle and self-interest: As Indians joined the fast-growing middle class, they would also become consumers of British goods and services.

In the short term, some call centres closed and some people were made redundant. Very rapidly, however, the Indian IT-services companies who were running the call centres for British companies—Infosys, Wipro, Tata Consultancy Services, Tech Mahindra, HCL and others—became investors in the UK, creating new call centres to benefit from the UK's skilled workers, diverse language communities and favourable time zone. At the same time, consumer preferences, the need for staff with local cultural familiarity and rapidly-rising staff turnover in the fast-growing Indian outsourcing sector, all contributed to decisions by many banks and corporate customers to bring customer-facing work back to Britain, while growing their technical and R&D capabilities in India.

It was, of course, much easier to make the argument for trade and to support individual workers and communities through the disruptions that trade can cause, at a time of sustained economic growth at home and abroad. Crucially, British trade unions, with their international outlook, also set their face against protectionism.

Today, in the long aftermath of the global financial crisis, making the argument is much harder. Although the UK unemployment is low and the numbers in work at a record high, real wages for most workers have fallen or stagnated, low productivity threatens future living standards and a growing proportion of part-time workers would much prefer a secure full-time job. As the Prime Minister spelled out in her Guildhall speech, shortly after returning from Delhi, 'Globalisation…has left too many people behind.' Government action, through a modern industrial strategy, is essential to spread the benefits of trade and globalisation to every part of the community.[2]

India has changed dramatically over the last twenty years. And so has its relationship with Britain. But what I heard on my first ministerial visit at the height of the dot-com boom in 1999—'Our connections are so close, the opportunities are so big, but we aren't doing as much together as we should be'—remains, frustratingly, the case today.

Investment, of course, is the big success story, in both directions. For nearly fifteen years, the UK has been the largest G20 investor in India, while Indian firms invest more in the UK than the rest of the European Union combined. Furthermore, at a time when trade between India and Germany has shrunk, the UK's has continued to increase, although not as fast as India's trade generally. None of us can be satisfied that the UK is no longer in India's top ten trading partners.

There are many reasons why bilateral trade has fallen short of the high ambitions set by political leaders. Britain—the world's second-largest exporter of services—faces a variety of restrictions on its legal, business and professional services in India. When it comes to education, one of the UK's largest export sectors and IT-enabled services, one of India's largest, the UK visa restrictions have created a perception in India that the UK is no longer welcoming.

More generally, British SMEs are less likely to be involved in exporting than, say, Germany's, while those that do export may see India as too difficult and risky.

Nonetheless, the opportunities for economic partnership between the two countries are compelling. On the one hand, India's scale, growth and demographics make it a market that no ambitious company should ignore. In less than three years, Narendra Modi has swept away many long-standing restrictions on foreign direct investment (FDI), even in sectors as sensitive as defence, while his strategy of 'competitive federalism' is accelerating state governments' moves to improve the ease of doing business. A recent UKIBC survey revealed that, as a result, six out of ten British firms with interests in India are likely to increase their investments.

On the other hand, Britain remains one of the most business and investment-friendly environments in the world. Despite the uncertainties inevitably created by Brexit, Nissan has recently confirmed a major new investment in its Sunderland factory and the government has emphasised that it will seek to maintain easy access to EU markets.

At a time of unprecedented technological change, India and Britain have more to offer each other than is sometimes recognised. Although Indians often see Britain as more 'heritage' than 'high-tech', the UK's world-leading science base and close partnerships between industry and academia should be a magnet for technology-hungry Indian investors. And Indians, with their centuries-old tradition of 'jugaad', have revealed an extraordinary capacity for innovation, giving India a world-leading presence in automobile components as well as its world-leading digital services sector.

Equally important, Britain and India have an 'installed base' of companies and people—including Britain's 1.5 million-strong Indian diaspora—that, along with a shared language and common legal systems, makes it easier to do business together.

With such strong foundations, it was encouraging that, at the suggestion of Liam Fox, secretary of state for international trade, the two governments agreed in November to undertake a comprehensive audit of the bilateral economic relationship. By the next Joint Economic and Trade Committee (JETCO) meeting in autumn 2017, the aim is to have a clear view of both opportunities and barriers. Both Dr Fox and his counterpart, Commerce Secretary Nirmala Sitharaman, are rightly keen to identify early wins, without waiting for Brexit. But the intention is also to clear the ground for a bilateral free-trade agreement (FTA) or comprehensive economic partnership agreement (CEPA) as quickly as possible after the UK leaves the EU.

Of course, the scope of an agreement will depend on the terms that are finally agreed for Brexit. If, for instance, the UK remains within the European Union Customs Union, then the tariffs we charge on goods imported from India or other international partners will remain unchanged.

India and the UK, however, are service-led economies and any new bilateral arrangements must reflect that fact. Unlike manufactured goods, which have traditionally dominated trade negotiations, trade in services has two unique characteristics. Increasingly, the product can be digitised, with legal research and the services of a personal assistant joining music downloads as the stuff of e-commerce.

But trade in services also means movement of people. It is vital to understand that what is at stake here is not permanent migration, but instead the temporary movement of people, buying and selling, delivering and consuming services. This includes the 330,000 Indians visiting the UK each year and the 800,000 British tourists to India (many of them encouraged by India's excellent online visa-on-arrival scheme), all participating in a sector that is vital to both economies. They may be brilliant Indian students coming to the UK universities and colleges, buyers and beneficiaries of one of our most important exports and also building people-to-people relationships that can last a lifetime. They may be Indian IT professionals coming to the UK for a few months or a year, helping to deliver IT-enabled services—a vital Indian export—that raise the productivity of British-based firms, and benefiting from corporate training here or, indeed, helping to train workers here.

In turn, these mobile service workers may be British lawyers, experts in international commercial law, who now take their services to Singapore, Hong Kong and Dubai and would like to offer them in Mumbai and Delhi, employing and training Indian lawyers and supporting Indian firms as they globalise. They may be British architects who are already contributing to the design and development of India's great cities but who could do so much more if they were allowed to establish offices in India.

Unfortunately, in British public debate, temporary movement of people has got muddled up with long-term migration. Even worse, visas are treated as if they were a completely different issue from trade. These confusions will have to be cleared up if we are to succeed in establishing the new economic relationship with India that could bring so much benefit to both countries. Both publicly and privately, Indian ministers and officials are absolutely clear that Britain cannot be a free-trader in goods but a protectionist in services. For at least two decades, India has consistently and rightly argued for liberalising 'Mode 4' (WTO jargon for trade in services through the temporary movement of people) and it will not abandon that position now. Nor should it. Trade in services—including temporary movement of people—was central to India's CEPA with South Korea, which Indian policymakers often point to as a model, just as it is to the new agreement between the EU and Canada that was strongly supported by the UK.

Brexit could provide the opportunity for a course correction. The referendum was won on the promise to 'take back control', including control of the UK's borders. PM May has made it clear that, whatever else is negotiated, Brexit will mean an end to the current system of freedom of movement within the EU. If that is accompanied by more effective exit as well as entry checks, intelligence cooperation to identify, exclude and remove those who threaten our security and firm action against overstayers and illegal entrants, it will create an opportunity for the British government to establish a new policy on labour mobility that will support growth, jobs and better living standards in Britain. (It could also allow a more generous and far-sighted policy towards asylum seekers.)

As the Prime Minister argued in her Guildhall speech, a modern industrial strategy is not about 'propping up failing industries or picking winners', it is about creating the conditions to generate tomorrow's jobs and tomorrow's businesses as quickly as possible. That requires far more effective support for people who are losing jobs, particularly where new technologies are transforming an entire sector or occupation. Together, government, educational institutions and employers need to ensure that British workers have the resilience and skills to take new jobs and set up new businesses. But a modern industrial strategy also involves bringing international skills and entrepreneurship to the UK—sometimes because there simply aren't enough local people with the right skills, sometimes because the incoming workers need the training and experience they will get in Britain and sometimes because they will themselves bring new skills and help to train local people. Most of all, these short-term movements are vital because in a global economy that is being transformed by new technologies, we need talent from all around the world to ensure that our companies, our universities and our public services are always improving and always innovating.

Trade negotiations inevitably involve give and take and, sometimes, very difficult compromises on both sides. But the UK and India will not be engaged in negotiations until after Britain finally leaves the EU, probably in March 2019. Between now and then, we have a unique opportunity for the two governments and the two business communities to create a very different understanding. It is vital, however, that the UK is not seen as reducing the relationship to something that is merely transactional.

The issue of student visas illustrates the point. From a narrowly economic point of view, Indian students coming to British universities are buying a British export; if their numbers fall, as they have dramatically in recent years, Britain's exports are damaged and our trade deficit increased. In the debate about student visas, however, it is the Indian government and Indian public opinion that is urging us to export more! Despite considerable efforts by British ministers and diplomats to persuade India that there is no limit to the number of qualified Indian students who will be accepted, the government's focus on overall migration numbers, together with restrictions on postgraduation employment—amplified in India's powerful public media— has created a real sense of bewilderment and hurt amongst India's policy and business elite. It is perfectly true that there is no cap on student numbers from India or anywhere else and, for that reason, removing students from the overall migration count would make no practical difference. (In any case, precisely because students only come for a short period, generally of a few years, the numbers leaving each year must roughly match the numbers arriving.) Nonetheless, a clear separation between students and other temporary visa-holders, and actual migrants, would send a powerful symbolic message and suggest that Westminster and Whitehall understand the emotional ties and tensions between the two countries.

Identifying and removing barriers to trade, whether before or within a comprehensive economic agreement, will be extremely important. But we can and must do more.

I welcome the fact that the UK now has a Department for International Trade (DIT), working closely with the Department for Business, Energy and Industrial Strategy, providing increased ministerial firepower for trade and investment issues. I also welcome the fact that ministers recognise the importance of outward as well as inward investment to British corporate success, in place of the somewhat mercantilist attitudes of their predecessors. The 'exporting is GREAT' campaign and new website reflect the new department's commitment to redoubling efforts to get more British businesses trading and investing internationally, especially in India and other high-growth economies.

British diplomats, together with UK Trade and Investment (now part of the new DIT), have always supported British business in India. The Prime Minister's initiative in taking a delegation of SMEs, rather than the leaders of large corporates, is very welcome. But despite many excellent examples of such support, there is a sense that many other developed countries give their businesses more backing. In Germany, for example, government-mandated membership of local chambers of commerce has created a powerful domestic and global network of business-led, professional organisations supporting German businesses to grow and globalise. Compulsory membership is unlikely to be tried in Britain any time soon, so we need to find other ways. The Italians, for instance, provide financial support so that an SME that simply doesn't have the necessary bandwidth can employ an experienced export manager to start opening up new markets.

In India, the UK–India Business Council has been backed by the British government to provide much stronger support to SMEs looking to enter or expand in India. UK Export Finance, also now part of DIT, has responded to business criticisms by substantially improving its offer. Government and business together need to raise the appetite of British firms to internationalise—ideally with a big, sustained marketing effort across all media and every organisation that SMEs come into contact with. Why not, for instance, add trade promotion material to the communications that HMRC (HM Revenue & Customs) already sends to SMEs? Thousands of British Indians are already doing business in India (and Africa) or are employed by larger firms to lead their efforts in India and South Asia. But far more should be done to build on those invaluable family ties across the wider diaspora community. With government, business and the wider community working even more closely in partnership, we have a unique opportunity for Britain to weave a powerful web of connections between entrepreneurs, businesses and consumers in both countries—to the great benefit of all.

Patricia Hewitt is Chair of the UK–India Business Council.

ENDNOTES

1. https://www.gov.uk/government/speeches/india-uk-tech-summit-prime-ministers-speech
2. https://www.gov.uk/government/speeches/pm-speech-to-the-lord-mayors-banquet-14-november-2016

Financing India's Growth— Opportunities for Infrastructure and Green Finance

NIKHIL RATHI

INTRODUCTION

India achieved the fastest economic growth rate in the G20 in both 2015 and 2016—over 7 per cent in both years. Ambitious long-term structural reforms are underway, which promise to underpin this growth trajectory. These include most notably the landmark agreement on a nationwide framework for Goods and Services Tax, and demonetisation. Far-reaching financial market reforms are progressing, in particular in relation to Indian corporate bond markets, public listing of Indian stock exchanges, further openness to international investors and gradual internationalisation of the Indian rupee. Crucially, to bolster economic growth and improvements in productivity, investment will be critical, particularly investment in infrastructure. The World Bank has estimated that the investment gap to be filled could be close to 10 per cent of India's GDP and the chairman of India Infrastructure Finance Co Ltd suggested that USD 750 billion would be required for India's infrastructure sector over five years. It is in this area in particular—supporting the financing of Indian infrastructure—that the global capital markets in London can play a role and bolster broader cooperation between India and the UK. And together we can take a lead in delivering global reforms, such as harnessing green finance for infrastructure.

London has a long history in the world of finance. In January 1698, a stockbroker named John Castaing pinned to the wall of Jonathan's Coffee House in the City of London the first-ever list of stock prices. Over the course of the last 315 years, that list, and the investors and brokers who must have crowded around it, became the London Stock Exchange and today, as then, it is the world's most international market, home to over 2,200 companies from across 115 countries.

London's role as the pre-eminent global centre and gateway for international investment has been its calling card ever since. Indeed in 1698, an investor passing Jonathan's Coffee House could have purchased 'India Stock' for 53 and three-quarter shillings. Today an investor would have the choice of more than fifty Indian companies to choose from, with a combined value of more than £100 billion (approximately 10 lakh crore rupees).

INFRASTRUCTURE FINANCE

London's role as the leading source of global capital for ambitious companies and countries was underlined by the landmark visit of Prime Minister Modi to the UK in 2015 during which he announced India's plans to tap the London markets for Indian-rupee-based financing—the masala bonds. This builds on London's position as the leading global foreign exchange centre.

Since then, London has become the foremost international market for offshore rupee-denominated debt—masala bonds, allowing Indian companies to raise money internationally without foreign exchange risk. In the last six months of 2016, over USD 1.1 billion (INR 7,500 crore or £900 million) of rupee-denominated bonds were issued in London. These included a series of pioneering and highly successful bond issuances from HDFC (INR 3,000 crore or £366 million) and NTPC (INR 2,000 crore or £244 million), which will pave the way for Indian corporates to raise significant quantities of finance in London. We also saw the Canadian province of British Columbia become the first foreign subnational entity globally to issue rupee-denominated bonds in a back-to-back transaction with HDFC. Supranational entities, in particular the International Finance Corporation (IFC) and European Bank for Reconstruction and Development (EBRD), continue to be an anchor for the market, including issuing rupee-denominated instruments for a tenor as long as fifteen years. This shows confidence in India's reforms, with global investors willing to take rupee currency risk over a long-term horizon.

Going forward, further issuances are anticipated from the National Highways Authority of India (NHAI) and Indian Railway Finance Corporation (IRFC), as well as other Indian entities, including Energy Efficiency Services Limited and the Indian Renewable Energy Development Agency, preparing to issue green bonds including masala bonds in London.

The funds raised so far and in the future are being used for a wide range of infrastructure projects in India ranging from renewable energy and housing to transport and rail. It will take time for the global masala bond market to deepen, but in the long term it should prove to be a resilient source of finance for India. The experience of the renminbi dim sum market in London provides useful context. London has now seen over 100 renminbi bond issuances, including the first-ever international RMB issuance by the Chinese government itself which provides an important benchmark. Chinese banks have also been important issuers and the Reserve Bank of India too has now permitted Indian banks to issue masala bonds. Notably, the dim sum market has evolved so that it is used by a wide range of global issuers from all parts of the world—Australia, Canada, Middle East, Asia and Europe. China is also now seeing a deepening of its onshore bond market, with a number of international issuers, such as the IFC and HSBC, issuing onshore in RMB in China through the 'panda bonds'.

The Reserve Bank of India has announced a range of steps to strengthen India's corporate bond market, including further quotas for international investors, reforms to the central bank's liquidity programmes and repo and currency markets. These are landmark reforms, which will further support international investment into India. And through global partnerships London Stock Exchange Group can provide the tools to make this investment a reality. Work is now underway between the State Bank of India and FTSE Russell, part of London Stock Exchange Group, to create an FTSE–SBI India Bonds Index Series to support the development of India's growing corporate bond market. Indexes such as this are the tools that will build investment in India, helping to create deeper pools of international liquidity in the sovereign and corporate bond market. As Arundhati Bhattacharya, chairperson of State Bank of India said, despite investor appetite to access India's ongoing growth story, Indian issuers' bonds do not have a credible global benchmark for passive investment funds to tap the Indian growth story. The FTSE–SBI Indian Bond Index will be a catalyst, providing a yardstick for attracting these funds into Indian bonds, thus supporting the crucial secondary market.

And over time we are looking to develop secondary market liquidity for masala bonds and other instruments from Indian issuers—so as to further improve transparency and price discovery and over the long term lower the borrowers' funding costs.

GREEN FINANCE

The green element to major infrastructure projects is gaining global investor attention and India will be at the heart of these developments. Over the coming decade, it is anticipated that several trillion dollars will be raised through green finance instruments, be they green bonds, green funds or green equities, with much of this for investment in India. In 2016, new green securities were launched by organisations around the world—from India and China to multinationals like Unilever, each taking advantage of a burgeoning pool of institutional capital invested through London dedicated to environmentally conscious investment. There is significant momentum behind green bonds—fixed-income instruments that are designed to help fund environment-friendly projects. Major global institutions, industry bodies and policymakers, including the G20, have backed the development of this market. In June 2015, London Stock Exchange became the first major exchange globally to launch a comprehensive dedicated green bond offering. To be admitted to London Stock Exchange's dedicated green bond segments, issuers are required to submit an external review document verifying the 'green' nature of the bonds. Ongoing disclosure and impact reporting are also encouraged to enable investors to make their own investment assessments regarding these instruments.

Recent research from the Global Sustainable Investment Alliance suggests that sustainable investing strategies now represent more than 60 per cent of professionally-managed assets for EU investors. These investors are attracted to Indian green finance instruments. Both NTPC (USD 300 million) and Axis Bank (USD 500 million) which issued internationally-certified green bonds last year for green infrastructure investment in India were, through these issuances, able to attract an even wider investor base than they had done before, including from Europe. These build on domestic issuances in India under SEBI's green bond framework. London has also seen a number of renewable energy funds raise money on the London market to finance operating investments in India, a trend expected to continue in the years ahead.

To build this market for India, five pillars are important:

1. Support green capital flows. This is already underway with the encouragement for green finance coming from the Indian government and SEBI. Indeed, the Indian railway minister has called for green finance to be at the heart of financing for Indian railways. New products may also be useful here and there is scope for regulators to provide further guidance. For example, in London last year, there was the first-ever issuance of a green covered bond by the Bank of China, connecting international investors to smaller issuers of climate-aligned bonds in mainland China. We have also seen the first climate-aligned pension fund, with the HSBC pension scheme incorporating climate risk alongside more traditional factors into the default equity fund managed by Legal & General Investment Management, with benchmarks provided by FTSE Russell.

2. Develop green infrastructure, particularly cross-border infrastructure. India is leading the way here. The Indian government has forecast that it will exceed the renewable energy targets set in Paris last year by nearly 50 per cent and three years ahead of schedule. Its latest ten-year energy blueprint predicts that 57 per cent of India's total electricity capacity will come from non-fossil fuel sources by 2027, ahead of the 40 per cent target by 2030 agreed upon in Paris.

3. Develop analytics and indexes to support the integration of climate risk into investment processes. For example, in June 2016, FTSE Russell launched its Green Revenues Low Carbon Economy data model, a groundbreaking data model that measures how listed

companies are transitioning to a low-carbon economy. This model enables investors to get exposure to the green economy and protect their investment from climate risks. The aggregate value of green revenues in FTSE Global Equity Index Series by market capitalisation is USD 2.9 trillion, approaching the USD 3.5 trillion market cap of emerging markets.

4. Data quality and standards. To improve global data flows between issuers and investors. The need for issuers to respond to demand for information from investors is clear and Indian exchanges and regulators can play a role here, perhaps through the UN Sustainable Stock Exchanges Initiative. By providing the information that investors want, Indian issuers can provide reassurance that they are effectively managing business risks and identifying opportunities. There is growing evidence that issuers that provide high quality information on the longer-term implications of environmental and social governance for their business are more likely to attract and retain long-term investors. These issuers can also reduce the cost of capital and increase their ability to raise new capital to finance sustainable projects. Further, having a clear view on these issues and strategies positions businesses at the forefront of opportunities presented by the unfolding sustainable and low-carbon economy.

5. Convening. Use India's position in the market to bring global alliances together. India, in particular, has an outstanding opportunity through its solar alliance with African and other countries to shape this market.

CONCLUSION

India provides some of the most exciting economic opportunities in the world. Financing those opportunities will be key to sustaining and increasing India's growth rate and productivity, particularly financing for infrastructure.

In the area of green finance, the next decade will be decisive: It depends on the investment currently being made on whether the world will stay on a two (or lower) degree path or tilt towards runaway climate change. The Green Economy transition is under way. This brings new risks, but also new opportunities, especially for India.

While similarities between today and the era of Jonathan's Coffee House remain, London Stock Exchange has clearly come a long way since 1698. Most significant though is the potential in the relationship between London and India. Like all relationships, for it to thrive, it will take continued focus and dedication by both parties, but it is clear that there is the will on both sides to build for the future.

Nikhil Rathi is CEO, London Stock Exchange plc, and Director of International Development, London Stock Exchange Group.

The Growing Influence of Indian Business on the UK Economy

Anuj Chande

Cast your mind back to April 1991—over a quarter of a century ago. The world was truly a different place in every sense. This was the year of the Iraq invasion into Kuwait and Russia's first free elections, and the first steps being taken to dissolve the USSR.

It was the year of the collapse of BCCI (Bank of Credit of Commerce International) and the deaths of Robert Maxwell and Freddie Mercury. The internet was made available for unrestricted commercial use and the use of computers worldwide reached 1 million only (2016 figures are 3.4 billion).

In India two significant events took place. In this year, Rajiv Gandhi was assassinated and the Indian Finance Minister, Manmohan Singh introduced a slew of measures to open up and liberalise the Indian economy after years of protectionism. The vision was to allow the world access (albeit restricted) to one of the world's emerging economies and permit Indian corporates to expand outside India.

It was on the back of this in 1991 that I saw a great opportunity from a UK angle to work on the India–UK corridor and set up Grant Thornton's South Asia's group with a particular focus on India. I vividly recall in 1991 when a number of Indian corporates—both large and small—took advantage of the globalisation opportunity offered by the economic liberalisation and decided to venture out. The UK with its historical, cultural and linguistic advantage was an obvious choice. Indian corporates set up offices in London and other parts of the UK, sought to form strategic partnerships with the UK counterparts and even make acquisitions. Rather disappointingly (and a lesson to be learnt and not repeated—see later), the UK corporates were in many cases a little wary or ignorant of what an Indian connection could offer. I remember acting for some emerging Indian technology businesses who had engaged us to identify strategic partners for them in the UK to help them to market and distribute their products. I found resistance to even meet with the Indian corporates let alone do any business with them. There was a perception of poor quality work and failure to meet deadlines and a general view that it was 'too difficult' doing business with Indians and the business opportunity was ignored. To our loss some of these same companies went to the US and other parts of Europe and are today truly thriving as successful global IT businesses.

Reflecting back on the twenty-five years, I would say that the UK corporate view on India remained much the same for a number of years and has only changed in the last fifteen years when India and its importance to the world economic order and the influence in the UK economy started to be recognised and truly accepted. This has been helped by the visibility received in the UK from the two major landmark acquisitions by Tata of Corus and Jaguar Land Rover in 2006 and 2008 respectively.

Whilst Indian investment in the UK dates back to 100 years when Tata first opened its office in London, it was really post-1991 that we saw a significant increase in Indian investment in the UK. Apart from certain periods when India was suffering from its own economic difficulties or credit crunch, Indian corporates became global and expanded through not only Europe but also USA, South America and even Africa.

INDIA MEETS BRITAIN REPORT—THE FIRST REPORT

Prior to 2014, there had been no research or information to show the full extent of the investment by Indian corporates in the UK. As veteran players in the market we decided it was time that we recognised the growing importance and influence of Indian corporates on the UK economy.

In collaboration with the Confederation of Indian Industry (CII) in 2014 whom we approached, we undertook new research to evaluate and quantify the growing footprint of Indian investment in the UK and their growing influence. The first report showed that there were in fact over 700 Indian companies in the UK employing more than 100,000 people[1]. There were also twelve Indian companies employing more than a 1,000 people. The India Meets Britain report provided a unique insight into the scale, business activities, locations and performance of Indian-owned companies making the biggest impact in the UK.

The first-year research highlighted that a lot of these companies were also fast-growing. In fact, in 2014 we identified forty-one Indian companies that had achieved more than 10 per cent growth and on a combined basis generated £19 billion turnover. The top five fastest growing companies had more than doubled turnover. Sector-wise, these fast-growth companies were spread 32 per cent in technology and telecoms, 22 per cent in pharmaceuticals and chemicals, 10 per cent in engineering and manufacturing, 10 per cent in automotive and the rest spread across other sectors such as logistics, energy and food. The regional footprint seemed to be evenly spread across the country with significant geographical bias. The report also highlighted that the Indian presence was through a mixture of greenfield projects as well as acquisitions.

India Meets Britain 2015 Report

The report for the next year showed that the number of Indian companies had jumped to 800 and whilst only thirty-six recorded growth rates of 10 per cent or more, they recorded a jump in combined turnover to £22 billion from £19 billion in the previous year. The three sectors that continued to dominate were technology and telecoms (42 per cent), pharmaceuticals and chemicals (22 per cent), manufacturing and engineering (14 per cent) and automotive (8 per cent). Region-wise they continued to be evenly spread through the country.

Employment-wise, employee numbers increased to 110,000 and the number employing more than 1,000 increased by one, to thirteen.

Given the radical shift in the public debate around taxation and the allegations of foreign companies not paying their fair share of tax we sought to quantify the amount of tax paid by Indian corporates and we estimated that Indian corporates were paying around half a billion pounds in corporate taxes and this number would be higher if you included employer taxes and sales taxes.

INDIA MEETS BRITAIN 2016 REPORT

The 2016 report showed that while the number of Indian companies in the UK grew slightly to 815, they continued to play a major part in the vibrancy of the UK economy. In fact, the number of companies growing by more than 10 per cent nearly doubled to sixty-two and they had a combined turnover of £26 billion. Sector-wise, the dominance of technology and telecoms and pharmaceuticals and chemicals continued with 32 per cent and 19 per cent respectively. Interestingly, for the first time we saw the financial services sector hitting the 10 per cent barrier. This had an impact on the geographical spread as it made London become more dominant with nearly 39 per cent of the fastest-growing Indian companies being based in the financial capital. Taxation-wise the corporate tax bill paid by Indian companies in the UK rose to £650 million from £500 million. On the employment side there was little growth on numbers and the net number of employees stood at 110,000.

THE EU FACTOR

In the 2016 report, we had highlighted the EU factor and impact on Indian investment. It is probably worth repeating what we wrote back in April 2016: 'Uncertainty surrounding the UK's impending EU referendum and the possibility of Brexit may have a bearing on both the UK economy and Indian companies' appetite for investing in the UK, particularly those seeking access to the European market. Potential Brexit is a pressing concern for companies considering the location of a European headquarters. Whether a London and a UK outside the EU will remain an attractive destination for Indian companies remains to be seen.'

Clearly it is still early days to understand what will be the real impact of the EU exit in terms of continued appetite of Indian companies coming to the UK. My own view is that it will be mixed and one needs to understand the main drivers for Indian investment in the UK. If you look at the historical drivers in the past which would continue for the future, they fall into three main categories, which are: Access to markets, brands and technologies or design.

For an Indian company whose main driver is access to only the UK market, Brexit should have no direct impact. Conversely, an Indian pharmaceutical company looking at using London as a launch pad to European market for its drugs may think twice. This is particularly relevant as hitherto the European drug licensing authority (MHRA—Medicines and Healthcare products Regulatory Agency) has been headquartered in London. Post Brexit, there are rumours that the authority may relocate to somewhere in Europe. However, for an Indian company that is looking to access the UK design and technology, there should be no impact. A classic example of this is Tech Mahindra's post-Brexit acquisition of a company called Target for its technology products for the leasing industry. Similarly, Indian corporates looking for iconic British brands to then leverage back to India and other emerging economies will be unaffected by Brexit. Even today, despite any European market access issues, I am sure Tata would still buy Jaguar Land Rover (JLR). Another aspect of Brexit that weighs on the minds of Indian companies is what the stance will be on future immigration into the UK for non-Europeans. There are concerns particularly within the Indian technology companies that work permits will become more difficult and; in fact we are already seeing signs that this is happening.

Interestingly, one of the side impacts of Brexit has been the 20-25 per cent devaluation of sterling. We have seen for ourselves an increase in interest of Indian corporates to seek the UK acquisitions on the back of the devaluation. This renewed interest seems to be across sectors.

A number of commentators have remarked that Brexit will now allow for a bilateral trade agreement between the UK and India. We are all aware of the huge time delay that has taken place with the EU–India treaty and there is hope that the UK–India trade agreement can be completed quickly. The issue will be as to when proper negotiations can start without getting the UK into legal difficulties with Brussels.

The exact nature of Brexit is also going to be important for India. For example, the Indian banks in London that are also interested in Europe are anxious to know what passporting rights London-headquartered banks will be allowed.

As the UK, we are very fortunate to have so many Indian companies here and we need to ensure we continue to attract them and highlight the benefits irrespective of whatever model emerges. We need to promote, for example, the extremely low rates of corporate taxes in the UK which are the lowest in Europe. For the Indian individuals who are here for limited periods, our unique residency/domicile taxation principle should continue to be attractive. We must also be proud of our skills and expertise in design, engineering, technology and financial services and ensure we continue to promote these. I also believe that the power and connections of the 1.5 million Indian diaspora have not been harnessed. There has been a lot of rhetoric in this area but it may be time to consider innovative ways of harnessing the connections and knowledge. A possible suggestion may be to identify individuals of Indian origin from the UK business community and appoint them and give them tools and status to be 'Business Ambassadors' promoting the UK to Indian corporates.

The Modi Factor

There is no doubt in anyone's mind that May 2014 marked a turning point in the political and economic landscape of India. The election of the Modi government was welcomed by all, whether it was the common man, the business community, the political class or the economists.

The previous government had put the country in political paralysis for a number of years and international confidence in India had suffered.

It is evident that the new government has made significant economic progress and there is still much to do. Many have remarked that not enough has been done and that the on-ground realities are still not reflecting the headline policies. The problem is that India is like a giant oil tanker that went seriously off course and the new captain on the deck needs to bring the oil tanker back on course and this takes time.

Assuming that the government is re-elected in the next election and is allowed to continue its reform programme, India is poised for significant economic growth and prosperity. This bodes well not only for Indian companies but also for the UK corporates who want to or should access the growing

Indian consumer base as well as the increasing manufacturing capability in India.

Generally, there is no doubt that a stable Indian government moving in the direction that Modi is taking is good news for the UK in many respects. A growing Indian economy with all its infrastructure and other requirements requires access to foreign capital. With London remaining as a financial capital of the world, there is a big role to be played by the UK. We have already seen this with the recent masala rupee bonds and the USD 1.1 billion raised since July 2016, and there is talk of revival of London equity markets for a share of the Indian pie.

The Next Twenty-five Years

Based on shared history dating as far back to the original East India Company and its trade and investment with India, the links between India and the UK should be the strongest in the world. While there is no doubt that Indian presence in the UK is significant but conversely the UK presence in India is not at the level to justify or reflect this historical heritage. There is a need to build on history and ensure that our connection with India is on a 'relationship' as opposed to 'a transactional basis'.

While there is no doubt that over five or even ten or twenty-five years' time the Indian corporates will remain a force in the UK economy, we need to not be complacent and not take it for granted. We must recognise and accept that India is going to be one of the largest and most powerful economies in the world and will increasingly have a greater choice over destinations for investment in the future. The UK and India have a lot to offer each other and we need to do our part to ensure that the relationship grows and does justice to our historical heritage with each other.

Anuj Chande is a Partner and Head of the South Asia group at Grant Thornton UK LLP.

Endnotes

1. May include overseas employees in the UK subsidiaries of Indian companies.

A Refreshed Outlook with Clear Trade Priorities—A Necessity

Rajiv Memani

Ahead of her visit to India in November 2016, Prime Minister of the UK, Theresa May is understood to have said that India is the UK's most important and closest friend and a leading power in the world, which is on the path of far-reaching reforms, led by Prime Minister Narendra Modi.

There are many synergies that support a stronger India–UK relationship, including democratic values, a common legal and administrative history, and English as the common language. The Indian community settled in Britain has helped strengthen the bilateral ties over decades. Today, India is the third-largest investor in the UK and the UK is the third-largest G20 investor[1] in India. However, the slowing down in bilateral investments in the last two years sets the stage for both countries to refresh their outlook and work more closely for improving trade, investment and economic collaboration in the coming years.

Strong Trade Partners

The UK is one of India's top trading partners. According to estimates from the Indian government, total trade value with the UK was worth USD 14.02 billion in 2015-16, of which USD 8.83 billion was in exports from India and USD 5.19 billion was in imports[2]. However, the percentage growth in total trade between the two countries has remained constant, with a marginal upward trend from FY10 to FY16.

Brexit has opened up opportunities for the two nations to negotiate trade deals. According to a research paper by the Commonwealth, titled 'Brexit: Opportunities for India', a free trade agreement between the UK and India would increase trade between the countries by 25 per cent. If implemented after Brexit, the UK's exports to India would increase by 50 per cent, from USD 5.2 billion to USD 7.8 billion. An actual treaty cannot be signed between the parties until the UK leaves the EU, but an interim understanding between the two countries is currently building up. In fact, Theresa May, during her visit to India, promised to lift all the trade barriers between the countries and offer several concessions to Indian business travellers to give a fillip to bilateral trade.

INDIA: AMONGST THE MOST INFLUENTIAL PARTNERS FOR THE UK

India has emerged as a strong player and a significant consumption and investment hotspot amongst the BRICS countries, being the fastest-growing economy in the world (GDP of 7.3 per cent[3] in FY15-16) and with the emergence of a new middle-class consumer market due to rising incomes. In 'Ready, Set, Grow: EY's India Attractiveness Survey 2015', 86 per cent of the seventy-seven British companies surveyed considered India's large and growing market an attraction for investment.

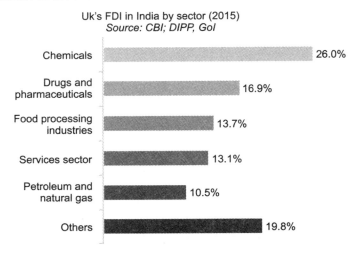

Uk's FDI in India by sector (2015)
Source: CBI; DIPP, GoI

Sector	Percentage
Chemicals	26.0%
Drugs and pharmaceuticals	16.9%
Food processing industries	13.7%
Services sector	13.1%
Petroleum and natural gas	10.5%
Others	19.8%

With a cumulative equity investment of USD 24 billion (April 2000-September 2016), the UK is the third-largest investor in India after Mauritius and Singapore accounting for around 8 per cent of FDI in the country for the period April 2000-September 2016[4]. However, FDI from the UK has been gradually declining since 2011-12 from USD 7.8 billion to USD 0.9 billion in 2015-16.[5] The UK investments into India are largely in the chemicals, drugs and pharmaceutical sectors. The other major sectors include food processing industries, the services sector, petroleum and natural gas.

Ease of Doing Business: A Key Requisite to Deepen Ties

India ranks 130 in the World Bank Group's Doing Business Ranking 2017, rising by a position over 2015 on account of the pro-investment reforms taken by Prime Minister Narendra Modi. India's ranking improved in two parameters: Securing an electricity connection and enforcing contracts. On the other hand, the UK's ranking has fallen by a position, from six to seven; however, it retains its ranking as one of the top countries in the G7 to do business, driven by the government's aims to cut red tape and reduce corporate tax[6]. The UK government's target is to be amongst the top five in the ease of doing business ranking, while the Government of India has announced its commitment to be amongst the top fifty within a few years.

Amongst the challenges cited by large UK companies looking to invest in India are: An inconsistent quality of infrastructure across the country, laws around land acquisition for mega/large-sized projects, the judicial system, an uncertain tax environment and high taxes, regulatory complexities for importing goods, corruption etc.

Several UK businesses have shared the need for replacing lowest-price bidding in tendering for government contracts with modern systems that consider and weigh cost, time, quality and performance in the selection process. The rigidity and lack of transparency around the payment terms and requirement of previous experience on similar projects have restrained their participation in the public sector. High tax cost associated with repatriating surplus cash from India to the UK has also been a deterrent. The effective tax rate (including corporate income tax and dividend distribution tax) amounts to approximately 48 per cent and has been cited as a dampener for the UK investors looking at India.

For small and medium-sized UK businesses, most of which are looking to test waters in new markets beyond the EU, difficulties and long timelines in unwinding Indian operations have often been mentioned as a challenge. The other hurdles include entry challenges, raising capital, human resource, asymmetric information on regulations and hindrances in technological access.

CHANGING INDIAN BUSINESS LANDSCAPE

Many of the investor concerns have been addressed by the Indian government since 2014 through an ambitious programme of regulatory and tax reforms. In fact, the UK investors have applauded the Indian government's eBiz initiative, which integrates various central government services to facilitate fast-track clearances and improve the overall business environment. The introduction of the Goods & Services Tax (GST) as a single tax structure is one of the biggest tax reforms undertaken by the government in decades and has been welcomed by investors globally. The passage of the Insolvency and Bankruptcy Code, 2016 has also been appreciated by investors, as it prescribes simplified exit procedures, enables time-bound settlement of insolvency and ensures a reliable and steady supply of credit.

The liberalisation of the FDI policy in sectors such as defence, rail infrastructure, construction development, insurance and medical devices, and simplification of procedures have also boosted the flow of FDI into the country since 2014. In fact, in 2015, India was the highest-ranked country by capital investment with USD 63 billion worth of FDI projects announced.[7]

On the tax reform front, the emerging trend of corporate tax rate reduction and base broadening in G20 economies can also be seen in both India and the UK. While the Indian government has committed to bring the tax rate from 30 per cent to 25 per cent over four years (beginning in FY17) along with proposals to rationalise tax incentives, the UK has recently legislated to cut its corporate headline rate to 17 per cent, which would give it the lowest rate in G20.

Reforms in India are taking shape at the state level too. Single-window systems have been implemented to grant all approvals required from state government agencies. Various state governments have also put in place grievance redressal mechanisms and investors have started feeling respite from procedural delays. Self-certification schemes for labour laws-related approvals, end-to-end online building plans and pollution-related approval systems are amongst many other initiatives undertaken by the Department of Industrial Policy and Promotion (DIPP) under India's Ministry of Commerce and Industry.

THE UK: AN ATTRACTIVE INVESTMENT DESTINATION FOR INDIAN BUSINESSES

The UK remains an important market for Indian companies with its competitive corporate tax rates, technology and telecommunications infrastructure, entrepreneurial culture, R&D incentives, wide range of government grants and a common language.

According to the latest figures released by UK Trade and Investment (UKTI) in their 2014-15 Inward Investment Annual Report, India undertook 122 FDI projects in 2014-15 in the UK, marking an increase of 65 per cent over the previous year and accounting for over 9,000 new jobs. These investments were primarily in the telecom, technology and pharmaceutical sectors[8]. The cumulative flow of Indian FDI in the UK during 2010-12 was USD 1.32 billion[9].

INDIAN BUSINESSES INVESTING IN THE UK DEALING WITH POST-BREXIT UNCERTAINTY

EY's Capital Confidence Barometer (CCB) 2015 showed that the UK has fallen out of the top five investment destinations for India for the first time in seven years. While the full impact of Brexit cannot be predicted as yet, pressure on investment clouds the UK's longer-term economic projects. For Indian business houses, the UK earlier served most often as a gateway to Europe, but with Brexit, this is changing. Possible increase in tariffs will impact competitiveness of Indian products and increase trade costs. This will require Indian businesses to rebuild their strategies for the UK market.

However, there has been an upside as well. The depreciation in the sterling exchange rate following Brexit has instilled interest in Indian companies to invest in the attractively-valued UK businesses and assets. That said, in order to ensure that the UK remains attractive for Indian businesses, the UK government needs to provide tax incentives and other financial incentives to Indian companies, and reduce regulations.

Besides the uncertainty around Brexit, the other challenges for Indian businesses looking to establish or expand operations in the UK have been stiff regulations on labour mobility, salary thresholds, tax payments, trading across borders and disclosures with regard to foreign worker employment ratios.

That said, both countries have taken steps towards learning from each other on the ease of doing business. For example:

- A memorandum of understanding (MoU) has been signed on ease of doing business, which will harness the UK's expertise to support India's efforts to climb the World Bank's Ease of Doing Business ratings.
- MoUs have been signed on intellectual property rights and ease of doing business towards sharing of best practices and technical assistance on certain parameters.
- A fast-track mechanism has been established to facilitate the UK's investments in India and for the UK companies in India and to set up an India–UK partnership fund under the National Investment and Infrastructure Fund (NIIF) to facilitate global investments through the City of London for Indian infrastructure projects.

Overall, in our discussions with business leaders in India, there is a strong appetite to invest in the UK for trade, technical collaboration and knowledge collaboration. Recently, both countries have taken significant steps towards bolstering this collaboration:

- The Newton–Bhabha Fund has been created with an increase in research collaboration from USD 1.25 million to USD 187.17 million in science and education.
- India has agreed to establish the India–UK Clean Energy R&D Centre on solar energy with joint investment of USD 12.2 million.
- A new antimicrobial resistance initiative with joint investment of USD 18.4 million is also being launched.

Enhancing Indian Talent Availability in the UK

An important factor to strengthen the bilateral ties and enabling ease of doing business is relaxing mobility and employment laws in the UK. This is significant as availability of educated, English-speaking Indian talent facilitates a sound understanding of work culture and geographical characteristics of both countries.

The number of Indian students enrolled in the UK universities has almost halved since 2011 from 39,090 in 2010-11 to 18,320 in 2014-15[10] due to stringent immigration and employment-related laws in the UK. Under the new norms, non-EU students after finishing their studies, must leave the country and apply for a work visa if they wish to return. An alternate mechanism may be devised to allow Indian students to participate in campus interviews. Similarly, a facility in the form of an employment exchange programme for students searching jobs in the UK and in neighbouring countries will help attract more students to the UK universities.

Sector-specific Opportunities for Bilateral Cooperation

TECHNOLOGY

Technology is emerging as the top investment sector for Indian companies in the UK. Since 2005, there has been a 133 per cent increase in tech companies investing in London, which accounts for 46 per cent of all projects[11]. Many India-headquartered businesses have applied for grants through Innovate UK, a UK government initiative to grant funding for projects in sectors such as manufacturing, ICT, automotives, food and health technologies and energy.

Even for the UK companies, India offers an attractive market with its more than 1 billion mobile connections and 350 million internet connections. Innovation-promoting policy initiatives such as Smart Cities, Make in India, Startup India and Digital India announced by the government in 2015 are creating a robust ecosystem for innovation and technology. British companies, along with capital, have immense potential to bring state-of-the-art technology and experience to India.

E-GOVERNANCE AND CYBERSECURITY

With their respective technology expertise, the two countries are strengthening their partnership on cyber and digital technology, including in support of India's Digital India initiative. The UK will provide advice on the setting up of the new Indian Cyber Crime Coordination Centre, and expert-level links will be developed between practitioners and policymakers in this field. The new MoU on e-governance will also build cooperation in bringing the benefits of a digital government to India's citizens. The two countries have also agreed to expand the UK's Chevening Cyber Scholarships programme for India and establish a Cyber Security Training Centre of Excellence.

FINANCIAL SERVICES

Britain-based fund managers have supported the development of the recent masala bonds in the Indian economy. Masala bonds allow an Indian issuer to raise money abroad without facing foreign currency fluctuation risks. This access to capital for Indian companies will ensure that the growing rupee bond market will continue to support India's ambitious infrastructure investment of USD 1.5 trillion.

DEFENCE

India has also opened up its defence sector for foreign investments and the UK is a leader in defence manufacturing. Identifying the opportunity to expand the UK's ties with India's defence sector beyond trade of defence equipment, the UK and India have signed several agreements where the UK will support the development of India's defence capabilities through technology transfer and joint research on new capabilities.

ENTREPRENEURSHIP

India's start-up ecosystem is budding with several promising ventures, and the Indian government is providing the necessary impetus to local entrepreneurship through initiatives such as Startup India, Stand-Up India etc. The UK has a more mature start-up ecosystem and can play an active role in supporting India in its start-up initiative by investing in large and mid-sized start-up enterprises. This would help create jobs and deliver critical services across several states. The Start-Up India Venture Capital Fund announced by Prime Minister Theresa May will support start-up enterprises and also promote additional capital for Indian start-ups from other investors, including the UK venture capital funds.

Way Forward

The UK investors are keen on investing in India, and the UK values India as a strategic trading partner going forward. Both countries are continuously working on ease of doing business and have taken some significant steps to address the concerns of global investors and strengthen bilateral ties. Brexit is indeed a significant incident for the UK to strengthen its special relationship with India and revive preferential bilateral trade and investment agreement.

While India needs to accelerate and implement its economic and tax reforms, the UK will have to address concerns around greater mobility and set clear trade priorities between the two countries.

Prime Minister Theresa May, during her visit to India, said that it is important for both countries to prioritise each other's priorities. That summarises the appropriate way forward for India and the UK to strengthen their bilateral bond.

Annexure I

TABLE I

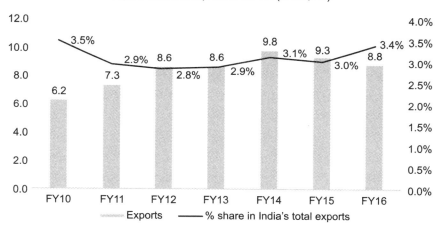

Figure 1: India's exports to the UK (in US$ bn)

Source: Ministry of Commerce and Industry, Department of Commerce, GoI

TABLE II

Annexure II

TABLE I

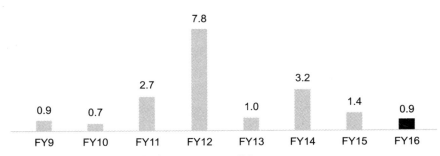

FDI Inflows from UK in India (in US$ bn)

Source: Department of Industrial Policy & Promotion, GoI

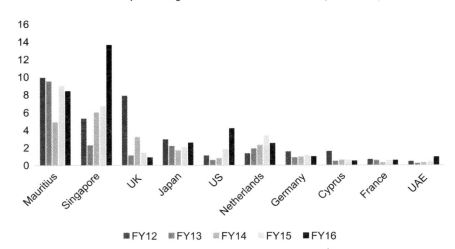

Share of top investing countries FDI inflows in India (US$ billion)

Source: Department of Industrial Policy & Promotion, GoI

ANNEXURE III

TABLE I

World Bank 'Doing Business' Ranking 2017

Parameters	Rank			
	UK		India	
	2016	2017	2016	2017
Overall	6	7	131	130
Starting a business	13	16	151	155
Dealing with construction permits	16	17	184	185
Getting electricity	15	17	51	26
Registering property	46	47	140	138
Getting credit	19	20	42	44
Protecting minority investors	5	6	10	13
Paying taxes	11	10	172	172
Trading across borders	28	28	144	143
Enforcing contracts	30	31	178	172
Resolving insolvency	13	13	135	136

Rajiv Memani is Chairman & Regional Managing Partner of EY India and Chairman of EY's Global Emerging Markets Committee.

ENDNOTES

1. Ministry of External Affairs, Government of India.
2. Refer to Annexure I, Table I, II for more details.
3. IMF Update.
4. Department of Industrial Policy and Promotion (DIPP), Government of India.
5. Refer to Annexure II, Table I.
6. Refer to Annexure III, Table I, for more details.
7. fDi Intelligence, a division of The Financial Times Ltd.
8. India meets Britain, Tracking the UK's top Indian companies by Grant Thornton & CII.
9. UNCTAD (United Nations Conference on Trade and Development).
10. Higher Education Statistics Agency.
11. London & Partners.

SOURCES

1. http://www.mea.gov.in/Portal/ForeignRelation/United_Kingdom_2015-07_27.pdf
2. https://www.hcilondon.in/pdf/Bilateral_Breief_oct26_2015.pdf
3. http://www.cbi.org.uk/news/uk-is-largest-g20-investor-in-india-at-22-billion-cbi-pwc/sterling-assets-india-uk-investment-creating-jobs-in-india/
4. http://www.imf.org/external/pubs/ft/weo/2016/update/01/
5. http://www.commerce.nic.in/eidb/

6. http://dipp.nic.in/English/Publications/FDI_Statistics/FDI_Statistics.aspx
7. http://dgft.gov.in/
8. http://dbie.rbi.org.in/
9. http://data.imf.org/?sk=9D6028D4-F14A-464C-A2F2-59B2CD424B85
10. http://www.cii.in/PublicationDetail.aspx?enc=1agwryCtEz7DIq63Mjvd75GxMJbJm0Vy63l5moA ru6s=
11. http://www.londonandpartners.com/media-centre/press-releases/2016/20160315-indian-tech-firms-look-to-boost-investment-in-london-following-visit-of-prime-minister-narendra-modi-to-uk
12. http://www.trademap.org/
13. https://www.gov.uk/government/news/uk-and-india-prime-ministers-trade-mission-and-bilateral-visit
14. http://www.ey.com/Publication/vwLUAssets/ey-2015-india-attractiveness-survey-ready-set-grow/$FILE/ey-2015-india-attractiveness-survey-ready-set-grow.pdf
15. http://www.ey.com/Publication/vwLUAssets/2016-UK-Attractiveness-Survey/$FILE/EY-UK-Attractiveness-Survey-2016.pdf
16. https://www.gov.uk/government/publications/ukti-inward-investment-report-2014-to-2015
17. http://timesofindia.indiatimes.com/business/india-business/India-becomes-3rd-largest-source-of-FDI-into-UK-as-investments-increase-65-in-2015-Report/articleshow/52042011.cms
18. http://economictimes.indiatimes.com/news/economy/foreign-trade/indias-investments-into-uk-more-than-doubled-in-2015/articleshow/52043466.cms
19. http://thecommonwealth.org/media/press-release/uk-india-bilateral-trade-deal-boost-uks-exports-26-billion
20. http://www.thehindu.com/business/Economy/uk-starts-trade-talks-for-postbrexit-deal-with-india/article8824943.ece
21. http://economictimes.indiatimes.com/news/economy/foreign-trade/uk-eager-to-have-free-trade-agreement-with-india-nirmala-sitharaman/articleshow/55296325.cms
22. http://www.thehindu.com/business/Economy/India-UK-Free-Trade-Agreement-may-be-easier-post-Brexit-CII/article14475965.ece
23. http://indianexpress.com/article/india/india-news-india/brexit-could-provide-fillip-to-india-uk-trade-ties-2881038/
24. http://economictimes.indiatimes.com/news/economy/foreign-trade/what-brexit-could-mean-for-india/articleshow/52831547.cms
25. http://money.cnn.com/2016/11/04/news/economy/theresa-may-india-trade/
26. https://www.theguardian.com/world/2016/nov/05/trade-uk-india-suffer-double-hit-theresa-may-visit-brexit-sterling
27. http://www.doingbusiness.org/data/exploreeconomies/india/
28. http://www.makeinindia.com/eodb
29. http://www.doingbusiness.org/data/exploreeconomies/united-kingdom
30. https://www.theguardian.com/business/2015/oct/27/britain-named-sixth-best-country-for-doing-business
31. http://www.telegraph.co.uk/finance/globalbusiness/11958263/Britain-overtakes-US-to-become-top-G7-country-to-do-business.html
32. http://www.doingbusiness.org/~/media/wbg/doingbusiness/documents/profiles/country/gbr.pdf
33. http://www.goinews.com/2016/11/07/india-uk-ink-mous-ipr-ease-business/

Making the Most of Tourism and Our Cultural Ties

Dr Jyotsna Suri

The year 2016 was unprecedented for the world economy. This was more so for the UK, as it marked the beginning of its exit from European Union following a historic referendum. The UK's desire to 'look beyond' Europe has accelerated its efforts to strengthen economic relations with its other major partners. In this context, the visit of Prime Minister Theresa May to India—her first visit outside Europe after assuming office—clearly highlights the importance the UK attaches to India as it resets its global relations.

India, which is also undergoing a metamorphosis, is today amongst the fastest-growing economies in the world. Its resurgence is reflected not only in its growth performance but also in its ability to set the agenda for global discourse in several areas. Backed by a series of economic reforms and policy initiatives under the leadership of Prime Minister Narendra Modi, the country is rapidly moving towards becoming a developed economy. These initiatives also provide avenues for investment and collaboration for other countries, including the UK.

In the joint statement issued during the visit of Prime Minster Theresa May to India, the two countries agreed to take a shared stake in each other's prosperity, generating jobs, developing skills and enhancing the competitiveness for both economies.

The relationship between any two nations cannot grow in the absence of a greater people-to-people connect. In the case of India and the UK, we already have a solid foundation to build on. Indian diaspora in the UK (approximately 1.5 million) is the largest ethnic minority community in the country and has been playing an active role in its social, economic and political landscape.

Indian culture and tradition has become mainstream in the UK, with great interest in Indian cuisine, cinema, languages, philosophy, performing arts, etc. The popularity of Indian cuisine in the UK can be gauged from the fact that tandooris, biryanis and samosas are sold at Marks & Spencer and Sainsbury's; Virgin Atlantic and British Airways serve curries on flights and 'chicken tikka masala' is often referred to as the UK's 'national dish'. Further, London's iconic Southbank Centre has hosted the Alchemy festival celebrating Indian culture for several years now and Hindi films regularly rank in the top ten grossing movies in the UK. The credit for this goes to various Indian organisations that have been actively promoting Indian culture by involving Indian diaspora as well as British organisations.

The most powerful sources of attraction in the UK for the young Indian population are its education, architecture, heritage and its cosmopolitan culture. India's historical connect with the UK resonates in the present-day institutions, universities and prominent buildings across several of its cities.

Tourism has also played an important role in the cultural exchange between the two countries. The United Kingdom has been the third-largest tourist-generating market for India in recent years. The tourist arrivals from the UK to India have grown from 798,249 in 2011 to 867,601 in 2015. Although this is encouraging, in terms of growth we see a CAGR of only 2.1 per cent as against 6.2 per cent for global tourist arrivals. Consequently, the UK's market share in India's overall tourist arrivals has declined from 12.7 per cent in 2011 to 10.8 per cent in 2015.

On the other hand, about 422,409 Indian tourists visited the UK in 2015, up from 355,472 in 2011, recording a CAGR of 4.4 per cent. This is in line with the 4.1 per cent growth in total tourist arrivals to the UK during that period. However, even India's market share in the UK's tourist arrivals continues to be low at 1.2 per cent. Another concern is that while Indian tourists' visits globally have grown significantly over the last decade, the UK's share in the total global Indian tourists' visits has nearly halved. In fact, France surpassed the UK as the most-visited European nation by Indians in 2015.

It is thus extremely important to strengthen our relationship in the fields of culture and tourism. This would enable both India and the UK to take their relationship to a new high, benefits of which will be seen in the realm of trade and investment.

For tourists, India offers immense options including magnificent mountains, beautiful landscapes, serene lakes and valleys, incredible beaches, vast deserts, enchanting backwaters and a rich history and culture embodied in historical monuments, palaces, forts, ancient architecture and archaeological sites. Its colourful festivals, folk music, dances, paintings, jewellery and handicrafts are a treat for the eye. In fact, India is also endowed with diverse flora and fauna, which has the potential to attract a huge number of tourists. The tourism potential in India is highly untapped and there is a need to actively focus on this sector.

In the UK, London is a major tourist attraction for Indian tourists and a large part of their spending is in this city. However, there are many more attractions in the country which could be effectively promoted. Promoting Britain outside of London should be the priority for the UK government.

Recognising the potential of tourism, the Indian government has introduced a series of schemes such as PRASAD (Pilgrimage Rejuvenation and Spirituality Augmentation Drive), HRIDAY (Heritage City Development and Augmentation Yojana) and Swadesh Darshan—development of domestic tourist circuits. Other measures include extending e-tourist visas to 150 countries, which has led to a quantum jump in the number of these tourist visas issued in recent times.

The British government has also undertaken several initiatives. In August 2016, it published the Tourism Action Plan, which includes a series of new initiatives and measures to help Britain outcompete other major tourist destinations. Through this plan and steps such as a new Discover England

Fund and revamped VisitBritain and VisitEngland campaigns, the country seeks to attract more tourist inflows.

The year 2017 will be celebrated as the India–UK Year of Culture. The year-long programmes, showcasing the innovative and exciting creative work from both countries will aid in building deeper cultural connections and spur tourist flows. British Library's South Asian archives would be digitised which would include Indian printed books dating back from 1714 to 1914. Two iconic British texts, Shakespeare's *First Folio* and the 1225 edition of *Magna Carta* would be travelling to India as part of the programme. A major exhibition at the CSMVS (Chhatrapati Shivaji Maharaj Vastu Sangrahalaya) museum would be the key attraction of the 2017 festival. Merlin group plans to invest around £50 million for setting Sea Life Aquarium and Legoland Discovery Centres across Indian cities, in addition to the Madame Tussauds planned in New Delhi.

The efforts taken by the two governments to enhance the people-to-people connect, strengthen cultural linkages and improve tourism are encouraging, but more is required to unlock the true potential. Steps underway should be complemented by policy initiatives to address the challenges converting them into opportunities through mutual cooperation.

While tourist inflows to India are on the rise and we have good connectivity into the country, internal movement in terms of infrastructure needs improvement. The UK can look at this as a potential area of engagement and support us in our efforts to improve last-mile connectivity through an integrated approach for transport systems.

The UK could also invest in development of identified heritage sites in India. Opportunities for investment for the UK also exist in development of port and related infrastructure that would provide impetus to cruise tourism. Some of the main destinations for cruise and boat vacations in India include Andaman Islands, Sunderbans, Goa and Cochin. Projects such as the Clean Ganga Campaign also provide an opportunity to be a part of river tourism, especially the Varanasi-Allahabad route and the Varanasi-Kolkata river cruise.

There is also a huge potential for boosting tourism by developing the amusement industry in India. The engagement, entertainment and leisure elements of tourism need to be blended at the tourist destinations.

We can also take cue from the UK's efforts to strengthen tourism infrastructure. Huge investment has been made in London's retail and leisure infrastructure. There have been continuous efforts to not only revive some of the old areas like Stratford, which saw a complete overhaul at the time of 2012 London Olympics, but also to strengthen the city's wide transport network and connectivity further. By 2018, the city is likely to see the introduction of Crossrail, which will connect East and West London. Similarly, Thames Clipper, introduced as a bus service on the River Thames, allowing sightseeing by boat, has now emerged as the fastest and most frequent service. The government is also working towards modernising the London Underground, London overground tube rail, trams and the Docklands Light Railways.

The city also offers travel ease and convenience to tourists. For instance, London Pass gives free access to more than sixty attractions around London. The London Travelcard is valid on all London public transport systems. Similar services can be introduced in key tourist destinations across India.

As for the movement of Indians to the UK, easier facilitation of visa, immigration and customs procedure is essential. While some steps have been taken to improve visa services for the business travellers, visa regime needs to be made simple, efficient and cost-effective for all travellers. Our authorities must remain engaged in this area. It will be good to see the cost of visa for Indian travellers being brought down this year as it will be a true reflection of Britain's commitment to India as a valued partner.

In addition to steps for better connectivity and easier mobility, I see a need for greater promotional and awareness campaigns in both countries. One of the ways this can be achieved is through greater collaboration in film shooting and production. Another way is through the launch of an international media hosting programme for wider dissemination of information on new and upcoming destinations on both sides. Additionally, theme-based festivals can be organised at various tourist locations inviting participation of students and youth from both countries. The UK should accelerate the pace of collaboration in such areas as several other European countries are actively seeking Indian tourists.

As the UK readies to leave the EU, there is anxiety the world over. From the tourism perspective however, there seems to be a sense of optimism.

This stems from the fact that the correction which has been seen in the value of pound sterling following the announcement of the referendum, has made travel to the UK more economical vis-à-vis other prominent places in Europe. However, there are some concerns with respect to movement of people for business and professional travel and these need to be mitigated.

I have always believed that tourism has a great power to bring countries and people together. As people travel, they understand each others' cultures and such exchange automatically paves way for greater trade, investments and economic development. I can say this from my own personal experience. I first visited the UK when I was eighteen and my husband Lalit at twenty-three trained for two years at Vauxhall Motors. After we got married in 1973, we continued to travel to the UK regularly. Our visits became more frequent when our four children chose to pursue their higher education in the UK universities. Today, I am proud to share that we have recently opened The Lalit London, which is housed in the erstwhile St Olave's Grammar School near Tower Bridge. The Lalit London is a perfect amalgamation of two great countries and cultures. The incredible Victorian architecture is replete with rich Indian silk, handcrafted furniture, chandeliers and artefacts, and offers distinct Indian hospitality and culture to the UK capital. It is heart-warming to see the local British guests respond spontaneously to the namaskar that they are greeted with.

Greater cultural and tourism ties will deepen the already strong bonds of friendship that exist between our two countries.

Highlighting the importance of travel and tourism in the overall progress and evolution of mankind, Mark Twain said—'Broad, wholesome, charitable views of men and things cannot be acquired by vegetating in one little corner of the earth all of one's lifetime.'

Dr Suri is the Chairperson & Managing Director of The Lalit Suri Hospitality Group.

Supporting India's Energy Quest—Civil Nuclear Cooperation

PROFESSOR NAWAL K PRINJA

I recall the evening of 13 November 2015 sitting in the cold Wembley Stadium listening to the prime ministers of two of the oldest democracies in the world—Narendra Modi of India and David Cameron of the United Kingdom—addressing a record-breaking crowd ever gathered to greet a foreign dignitary in England. Both leaders outlined a great future their two countries can build together and, as the crowd applauded and agreed with their positive message about future collaboration, I could not help think of the many opportunities that lay ahead. There are several big challenges facing the world and without doubt one of the biggest is how to produce clean sustainable energy to meet the aspirations of millions.

On one hand we have the United Kingdom where the world's first commercial nuclear power plant was built in 1950s and such is the maturity of this industry in the UK that nearly all of the nuclear power plants with the exception of one will be shut down by 2030 as they reach the end of their design life. And on the other hand we have India that is embarking on a programme to build an array of new nuclear power plants trotting the path that the UK has already traversed. The opportunity to collaborate could not be any clearer. It is driven by the global need to have cleaner, sustainable forms of energy.

NEED FOR CLEANER ENERGY—A SHARED TARGET

In 2013, the UK government declared in its nuclear power strategy that nuclear energy has an important role to play in delivering the long-term objective of a secure, low-carbon, affordable, energy future. It also identified significant challenges that need to be met, both in the short term and for the longer term, to 2050 and beyond. The UK wants to maintain options for nuclear power making a major contribution to the longer-term energy mix. To achieve these objectives, it has identified three key enablers—research and development, skills development and international collaboration. The strategy goes on to acknowledge that the UK cannot act alone in aiming to realise the government's long-term vision but must work with others to provide a positive and informed political environment both domestically and globally. For capital-intensive nuclear projects it is prudent to collaborate both in the research and deployment of new technologies.

Currently, the UK has fifteen nuclear reactors generating 9.5 GWe producing about 21 per cent of its electricity. One of the scenarios being considered in the UK is to build the next generation of nuclear power plants that could produce nearly 30 to 40 per cent of the power by 2050. India has an equally ambitious nuclear power programme and expects to have 14.6 GWe nuclear capacity on line by 2024 and 63 GWe by 2032. With twenty-one nuclear reactors in operation, six under construction and further twenty-two units planned, India is definitely racing ahead to generate more nuclear energy. It aims to supply 25 per cent of its electricity from nuclear power by 2050. India's state-run Nuclear Power Corporation of India (NPCIL) is in talks with the French company EDF for building six Light Water Reactors (LWRs). It is the same design that the British government has recently approved to be built at Hinkley Point C. These six LWRs are to be built at Jaitapur in Maharashtra in India and with a capacity of 1650 MW each. Once complete, it will be the largest nuclear power plant in the world. Negotiations are also going on with the US-based Westinghouse which is expected to build another six units of 1,000 MW each in Andhra Pradesh. Looking at the scale of the new nuclear build projects in both countries, I am reminded of the words of David Cameron that 'both countries were united by the scale of their ambition'.

India has come a long way since the 1950s. The performance of India's nuclear plants is among the best in the world but they contribute only about 3 per cent of the total electricity production whereas in the UK 21 per cent of energy comes from its nuclear power plants. As India's economy grows, the demand for power will grow as there is a direct correlation between per capita GDP and electricity consumption. On top of meeting the increase in demand for electricity, India must meet its obligation to reduce emission of greenhouse gases. It is estimated that it may take thirty years before India would be likely to see any reduction in carbon dioxide. There is an urgent need to rely on cleaner forms of energy and as pointed out earlier, India's ambition is to achieve it by increasing the nuclear contribution to 25 per cent by 2050. The UK, like other countries, has similar obligation to reduce its carbon emissions.

India has a vision of becoming a world leader in nuclear technology due to its expertise in fast reactors and thorium fuel cycle but these technologies are not ready yet. Meanwhile, India needs to have 700 GWe energy generation capacity by 2032 to meet its 7-9 per cent GDP growth which will include 63 GWe of nuclear power. The target for nuclear power has been changing. In 2004, it was 20 GWe by 2020, but in 2007 the Prime Minister wanted it to be 'doubled with the opening up of international cooperation'. Whichever target we take, the fact is that India will require substantial uranium imports and international collaboration.

There are compelling reasons for more liberal civil nuclear trade between India and the UK. Adversaries to such a trade deal will point out several barriers. For example, India is outside the Non-Proliferation Treaty (NPT); there is no clear distinction between its civil nuclear power and atomic weapons programme and there remain concerns about nuclear liability insurance in case of an accident. All these barriers can be overcome and the Government of India has already taken steps in the right direction. The first step is to build mutual trust and for that it is pertinent to look at the past history of nuclear collaboration between the two countries.

The First Nuclear Reactor in Asia was Built in India

Historians will confirm that the seeds of Indian atomic research were first sown in the UK in late 1940s. Dr Homi Bhabha, the first chairman of the Atomic Energy Commission of India was trained in the UK. Sir John Cockcroft and Dr Bhabha collaborated to lay the foundations of atomic energy in India. Dr Bhabha also set up a laboratory called the Atomic Energy Establishment, Trombay which was later named the Bhabha Atomic Research Centre (BARC), where India's first nuclear reactor went critical on 4 August 1956. This was the first nuclear reactor in Asia and the fuel was provided by the UK. The reactor was kept in a water tank (swimming pool) to keep it cool and aptly named 'Apasara'. The name comes from a combination of two Sanskrit words: 'apa' meaning water and 'sara' meaning moving or living. So anything that lives or moves in water is 'apasara'.

In the same era, the UK was the world leader in civil nuclear power. World's first industrial-scale commercial nuclear power station was built in the UK and opened by HM Queen Elizabeth II at Calder Hall in Sellafield in 1956. However, the world ratings have now changed. According to the data published by International Atomic Energy Agency (IAEA), in 2015, the UK stood ninth in the league table of nuclear power producers while India was at the twelfth position. It is only through collaboration and mutual trust that both countries can rejuvenate the old nuclear ties and help each other to retain and even improve their positions in the league table of nuclear power producers.

India's Unique Three-stage Plan

The key to India's nuclear power growth is to develop reactors and a fuel cycle that is based on thorium which is plentiful in India. To achieve this, India has a three-stage uranium-plutonium-thorium plan. Stage 1 of the plan employs the indigenous Pressurised Heavy Water Reactors (PHWRs) fuelled by natural uranium which is imported. It will require modern Light Water Reactors (LWRs) from other countries as the spent fuel from them can be used to extract plutonium. Stage 2 uses the Fast Breeder Reactors (FBRs) that burn the plutonium to breed Uranium-233 from thorium. Under appropriate radiation conditions in an FBR, thorium can be converted into uranium. In stage 3, Advanced Heavy Water Reactors (AHWRs) will burn the Uranium-233 thus completing the fuel cycle that can help India achieve its ambition of a 25 per cent nuclear contribution by 2050 giving it a sustainable and secure supply of clean energy for the future. India is the only country in the world that is building technology to use all three materials—uranium, plutonium and thorium. The British nuclear industry can play a significant role in this development as it has world-class experience and capability in the design, construction and operation of nuclear plants and in full fuel-cycle facilities.

TRADE BARRIERS AND CHALLENGES

One of the stumbling blocks to India's civil nuclear power growth has been created by China that has indicated its unwillingness to support India's attempt to enter the Nuclear Suppliers Group (NSG). The NSG is a group of nuclear supplier countries that seek to prevent nuclear proliferation by controlling the export of materials, equipment and technology that can be used to manufacture nuclear weapons. China is blocking India's entry in the elite group on the grounds that NSG's rules disallow a member that has not signed the NPT. India's position is that it would not surrender its national interest by signing the accord, but wants its track record of non-proliferation to be considered as it does meet the intent of the NPT, therefore, it is entitled to join the NSG. India was granted an NSG waiver in 2008 that allows it to engage in nuclear commerce, but it does not have a vote in the organisation's decision-making. This waiver to the trade embargo was agreed upon by the NSG in recognition of India's impeccable non-proliferation credentials. India has always been scrupulous in ensuring that its weapons material and technology are guarded against commercial or illicit export to other countries. India will do its best to convince China and if the Chinese objection remains, all the signs are that India will continue and should continue with its plan to expand its civil nuclear power capacity to produce electricity.

Another trade barrier that is of concern to the vendors of nuclear technology is the lack of clarity about India's nuclear liability laws. India's 1962 Atomic Energy Act says nothing about liability or compensation in the event of an accident. Also, India was not a party to the relevant international nuclear liability conventions (the IAEA's 1997 Amended Vienna Convention and 1997 Convention on Supplementary Compensation for Nuclear Damage—CSC). Private-sector ownership of nuclear power stations is not yet allowed. All nuclear power plants in India are owned by NPCIL and

BHAVINI (Bharatiya Nabhikiya Vidyut Nigam Limited) both of which are public-sector enterprises, so the liability issues arising from these installations are the responsibility of the central government. In September 2008, Indian government assured the USA that India 'shall take all steps necessary to adhere to the Convention on Supplementary Compensation (CSC).' In January 2016, the Indian cabinet asserted that 'international and domestic concerns' over India's liability laws had been resolved with the 2015 establishment of the India Nuclear Insurance Pool. There are also calls to have full separation of civil and military facilities and setting up of an independent nuclear regulator. The Indian government announced in 2011 a plan to establish a new independent and autonomous Nuclear Regulatory Authority of India that was to subsume the present Atomic Energy Regulatory Board (AERB) which acts as the nuclear regulator.

INNOVATION FOR FUTURE

Political will can help overcome the aforementioned trade barriers. They can and should be overcome to exploit new opportunities to develop innovative technologies. One of the areas where India has already raced ahead of the UK is in Fast Breeder Reactor (FBR) technology. Construction for a 500 MWe Prototype Fast Breeder Reactor (PFBR) was started in 2004 at Kalpakkam near Madras. It was expected to be operationalised by the end of 2010 and produce power in 2011, but this schedule is delayed significantly. According to some reports, in June 2015 BHAVINI was 'awaiting clearance from the AERB for sodium charging, fuel loading, reactor criticality and then stepping up power generation.' Even though the project has suffered some delays, the sodium coolant is expected to be loaded in near future and the reactor is expected to go critical late in 2017 with commercial operation in 2018. Britain also has a need for an FBR which can be put to good use by burning the stockpile of nearly 100 tons of plutonium which is costing millions of pounds to store. The UK used to be active in research and development of FBR but that project has stalled and almost all of the FBR-related information lies dormant in its archives. Collaboration in development of FBR, where India has definitely taken a lead, is another opportunity worth considering.

Small Modular Reactor (SMR) technology is another area ready for development and exploitation. SMRs are ideal for a large country like India, especially for strategic remote areas where there are no grid connections. The UK government is currently running a competition to fund development of an SMR which is clearly aimed at deployment in the UK and other countries. In addition to the SMRs, a much smaller and safer micro SMR like the U-Battery concept is worth considering for further development and even first deployment in India. This Urenco-owned technology is not fully developed but India is hungry for new technology and with the world's largest number of English-speaking engineers and scientists, it is the right place to further develop innovative technologies.

Conclusion

The opportunities for civil nuclear trade are ripe. The UK needs India as much as India needs the UK. We hope that the new UK policies emerging after the Brexit vote will help to foster relationships, remove barriers and create opportunities for British companies to offer their expertise in developing India's civil nuclear plants. The UK government, in its long-term nuclear energy strategy, has declared an intention to enhance strategic relationships with India to help realise these opportunities. A host of new business opportunities exists in the field of civil nuclear power. If the aforementioned political and commercial concerns are removed, there can be immediate collaboration between the UK and India on a range of civil nuclear projects including development of FBRs, SMRs and micro SMRs that can usher in a new era of safer, cleaner and sustainable energy sources. As Dr Homi Bhabha had said in his presidential address at the first International Conference on the Peaceful Uses of Atomic Energy back in 1955, 'For the full industrialisation of the underdeveloped areas, for the continuation of our civilisation and its further development, atomic energy is not merely an aid; it is an absolute necessity.' The time has come for India and Britain to build on their nuclear legacy and work together for one glorious future.

Professor **Nawal K Prinja** is Technology Director of Clean Energy, AMEC Foster Wheeler.

An Unbeatable Combination in Legal Services

RICHARD GUBBINS AND GOPIKA PANT

India and the United Kingdom are often seen as sharing a historical partnership which as stated by the Indian prime minister is an 'unbeatable combination'. India with its diverse demographics, with almost 1.3 billion people where 70 per cent of the population is said to be below the age of thirty-five, 31 per cent born after the year 2000 and 70 per cent living on USD 2 per day, requires a robust and dynamic judicial system and judicial techniques to ensure freedom, justice and equality as enshrined in the Constitution of India. For various reasons, ranging from a bursting population to diverse social and religious practices, we find that at times India is caught in a zone in which it cannot provide affordable, transparent and equal justice to all and yet has the highest growth rate and a swiftly-changing economic landscape with the legislative estate of India taking a proactive approach to ushering in life-transformational reforms.

800 years ago, *Magna Carta* and the rule of law was born in the UK and this is now enshrined in the legal systems of many jurisdictions throughout the world. The UK has had a long history of being a great trading nation, and laws, policies and regulations throughout the centuries have always played 'catch-up' with business and the way people interact between themselves in

business and commerce. Many Britons came to feel that whilst the European Union (EU) promoted free trade and a common market, the bureaucrats in Brussels have stifled that with too much bureaucracy, over-regulation and creating jobs, mainly for themselves.

The UK is now in a position to reassert its sovereignty and to control its own laws, borders and regulations, to cut the red tape that has fettered business and commerce for so many years, to introduce policy and regulation that will help and facilitate the trade with India, to enable its own and Indian regulators to form stronger bilateral relationships and to employ 'best practices' outside EU rules. India will find it much easier to negotiate trade deals with the UK alone as opposed to with the entire EU bloc.

The EU referendum has given the UK and its people a much stronger feeling about their own identity and there is a new-found confidence that we are beginning to see in the UK business and commerce, something that the doomsayer economists are failing to recognise on a daily basis. This has to be good news for the UK's relationship with India. English law will remain the choice of law for many people. We only need to look at how many Russian-related cases are now being heard in the High Court in London. English law in international arbitration will increase and this will benefit India and Indian lawyers as India sets up more and more international arbitration centres within international finance centres such as the Gujarat International Finance Tec-City (GIFT) in Gujarat.

English regulators have demonstrated their prowess outside of the EU and we only have to look at the fine of GBP 670 million imposed in January 2017 on Rolls Royce following a deal reached between the UK's Serious Fraud Office, the Department of Justice and the regulatory authority in Brazil. The UK and India are now in a wonderful position, given their respective experience to help each other with the introduction of 'best practice' policy and regulation that will facilitate the trade in goods and services between our two countries. Together, the UK and India can ignore the bureaucratic excesses of the past which we have seen with Sarbanes-Oxley (which was criticised for being overregulated by government and its ineffective implementation) and the monolith that exists today in Brussels. Donald Trump is right in saying that there has never been a better time for the UK to do a deal with the United States of America and the same goes for India—'There has never been a better time for the UK and India to form an even stronger bond and relationship between the two countries.' Will Jaguar Land Rover (Tata) get a better tariff deal in the US than in Germany—we shall see! Our editorial is that 'business should get on with it and regulators should get savvy.'

Post Brexit, the UK will be free of European regulations and able to organise its relationships on a bilateral basis with international partners with complete sovereignty to legislate, enter into bilateral treaties and have a business environment most friendly to its businesses, and their clients and customers. In this light, India and the UK must aim to take their unbeatable combination to new heights. The legal communities of the two countries must also take path-breaking initiatives and support each other on the same, in the same manner as the UK has been a leading partner to Singapore in supplying judges for the Singapore International Commercial Court, assist in certain areas which may not have been tested in India as yet, given that the economy is young and evolving at a rapid pace, especially in the financial services and financial technology sectors.

Further, post Brexit, neither the UK nor India would be constrained to offer the same terms of legal initiatives to other European nations, thereby assisting each other to access competitive talent from their respective countries.

The Indian cabinet has given its ex-post facto approval to a memorandum of understanding (MoU) signed between India and the UK in November 2016, on ease of doing business in India. The MoU would enable exchange of officials from both the governments to facilitate sharing of best practices, offering technical assistance and enhanced implementation of reforms. Further, the collaboration is also expected to cover Indian state governments in its ambit.

Importantly, the UK government has shown interest to offer expertise in various areas such as insolvency, construction permits, risk-based framework for inspection and regulatory regimes, competition economics, getting credit, drafting laws and regulations reducing stock and flow of regulation and impact assessment of regulations. Moreover, recent high-level meetings between the officials of the UK and India, including between the prime ministers of both the countries, have set up the foundation for several new initiatives between the two countries, such as, a new Defence and International Security Partnership, MoU on intellectual property, initiative in relation to acceleration of financing investment in Indian infrastructure, issuance of rupee-denominated and masala bonds in London and so on.

While currently, India is ranked at 130 out of 190 economies,[1] the UK government has achieved phenomenal improvement in ease of doing business rankings in recent years. In light of this, the collaboration is expected to expedite adoption of innovative practices by the Government of India (GoI), state governments and their agencies leading to easing the regulatory environment in the country and fostering a conducive business climate in India. There is no question that such a partnership would be best supported by the legal professionals in both countries especially given that several expertise heads offered by the UK are related to law, rules and regulations and their enforcement.

India has the second-largest lawyer population in the world of approximately 1.3 million, with another 80,000-90,000 lawyers graduating from Indian law schools each year. While the global legal services market stands at approximately USD 593.4 billion (2015 figures), the generally-accepted figure of India's share in this is barely less than 1 per cent. With approximately 900 law schools of which eighteen are National Law Schools, one would expect India to have a far greater share of the global legal services market. It is instructive to examine some reasons for this. By keeping a closed door to the free flow into the legal services sector, India has denied its lawyers in-country exposure to what top international law firms offer in training and work environments. In fact, given its huge workforce of lawyers and an expanding graduating class every year, India could be exporting top-notch legal services to service the international community. Instead, a handful of lawyers leave the country for international practice each year causing a brain drain in the legal fraternity. They get these benefits outside India but rarely find appropriate opportunities to come back and work in the legal services sector in India.

Further, the Indian judicial system has, inter alia, been plagued by issues relating to (i) lack of speedy dispute resolution, (ii) lack of transparency and

(iii) low cost-effectiveness; all of these are actually a contradiction to the large number of lawyers available in India.

First, as per the Ministry of Law and Justice, Government of India, there are approximately 30 million pending cases before the Indian courts.[2] Among other reasons, such backlog is attributed to vacancies in the judiciary and slow civil and criminal procedures. According to the Law Commission of India (LCI), the situation of injustice created by such pendency and unwarranted judicial vacancies is egregious in commercial disputes where cases remain pending for years.[3] International investors and corporations consider such pendency as one of the biggest hurdles of resolving disputes in India and 'think twice' before investing or expanding their investment into India.

Second, the Indian judiciary has been facing the issue of lack of transparency in terms of appointment and transfer of judges. Appointment and transfer of judges in the higher judiciary is decided by a collegium of judges of the Indian Supreme Court, that is, judges appoint judges, which is not a known system of appointment in any developed country. The said collegium system has been strongly criticised, inter alia, due to non-disclosure of discussions and criteria adopted in recommending judges for appointment.

Third, litigation in India has become an expensive exercise. There are no set rules in relation to charge out fees by lawyers for rendering legal services and therefore, lawyers demand fees arbitrarily in this regard.

In light of the above, GoI has recently taken several progressive steps to tackle the aforesaid issues. For example, the National Judicial Appointments Commission Act, 2014 (NJAC Act) was enacted to replace the collegium system with the National Judicial Appointment Commission system. The NJAC Act provided for a transparent system of appointment and transfer of judges in the higher judiciary. However, the NJAC Act was held to be unconstitutional and therefore, struck down by the Indian Supreme Court in *Supreme Court Advocates-on-Record-Association and Anr. v. Union of India*.[4] Thus, the issue relating to appointment and transfer of judges continues to be a concern for the Indian judicial system.

The GoI passed the Commercial Courts, Commercial Division and Commercial Appellate Division of High Courts Act, 2015 (Commercial Courts Act) to establish certain commercial divisions and commercial appellate divisions in High Courts, and commercial courts at the district level to adjudicate commercial disputes of specified value and related matters thereto to effect the enforcement of contracts and improve efficiency in commercial transactions.

It is in this context that arbitration may be presented as an effective dispute resolution method which seeks to provide efficient and cost-effective alternative to the court system. The UK with its centuries of experience in dealing with cross-border and domestic commercial disputes is best placed to assist the Indian judicial system to overcome the problems it is currently facing in helping with training and the cross-border transfer of know-how and expertise.

On 8 October 2016, GoI launched the Mumbai Centre for International Arbitration (MCIA) in Mumbai, India. MCIA is India's first-of-its-kind international institution of arbitration and has essentially been set up with the aim of attracting resolution of disputes involving Indian parties, trade and investment into Mumbai and Maharashtra. MCIA is also an attempt to rationalise institutional arbitration in India and make India a global hub for international commercial arbitration.

While examining the efficacy of the MCIA, it is important to consider the development of arbitration, institutional arbitration in particular, as a method of dispute resolution in India and explore the possibility of the MCIA becoming a global hub for international commercial arbitration vis-à-vis other competing international institutions of arbitration such as the Dubai International Arbitration Centre (DIAC), the Hong Kong International Arbitration Centre (HKIAC), the Singapore International Arbitration Centre (SIAC) and London Centre for International Arbitration (LCIA).

Since the MCIA seeks to become a global hub for international commercial arbitration, we examine the possibility of achieving the same by comparing MCIA and its features with those of competing institutions.

Competing institutions are located at commercially-strategic locations that have facilitated their success in their respective regions. In the recent past, Indian parties seem to have preferred competing institutions. For example, according to SIAC's annual report, almost 30 per cent of the disputes heard by SIAC in the year 2015 were related to matters involving Indian businesses. It has also been observed that competing institutions have pro-arbitration and less interventionist judiciary.

For India, the MCIA seeks to provide an effective solution to the inherent issues of dispute resolution and may in due course prove to be an attractive institution for resolution of international commercial arbitrations as it seeks to provide cost-effective redressal to the parties vis-à-vis competing institutions.

However, to be a truly global or regional arbitration hub, India must endeavour to look to attract disputes without a specifically-Indian element and this can be mainly achieved by attracting top international professional talent to work in India including lawyers and international arbitrators.

From a global perspective, it is important to note that the GoI has recently taken up several initiatives under its 'Make in India' initiative to attract global investors into India. An increased number of global investors would attract more international commercial arbitrations as its necessary corollary. It is in light of this perhaps that the GoI has recently, in early January 2017 permitted international law firms to set up offices in special economic zones and international financial services centres such as the GIFT, in India in order to provide comfort to international companies to have their international legal advisers by their side while they work through and negotiate complicated cross-border contracts which have the potential to affect global business strategies which are often known only to trusted advisers.

Union Finance Minister Arun Jaitley has called for setting up of a task force of experts from BRICS nations to explore an effective and credible international dispute resolution mechanism.[5] He further called for the creation of a pool of arbitrators and arbitration lawyers of international repute among BRICS nations. He also stated that such mechanism may be extended to non-BRICS nations over the course of time. However, given the 'unbeatable combination' between India and the UK, collaboration between the two countries in the legal services sector would support India's efforts to transition into the next decade as a country which is empowered to deliver justice in a speedy, transparent and accurate manner for the benefit of all its citizens.

Richard Gubbins is Senior Corporate Partner of Ashurst LLP and Head of the Ashurst Business Group.

Gopika Pant is the Managing Partner of Indian Law Partners.

ENDNOTES

1. Doing Business Report, 2017.
2. Press release dated 3 March 2016 and issued by the Ministry of Law and Justice, Government of India, http://pib.nic.in/newsite/erelease.aspx.
3. Report No. 246 on 'Amendments to the Arbitration and Conciliation Act 1996'.
4. (2016) 5 SCC 1.
5. Valedictory Address at the Conference on 'International Arbitration in BRICS: Challenges, Opportunities and Road ahead' held on 27 August 2016, http://pib.nic.in/newsite/PrintRelease.aspx?relid=149266

Index

Contributors

 Ranjan Mathai was India's Foreign Secretary from August 2011 to July 2013. Graduating from the University of Poona in 1974, he spent four decades in the Indian Foreign Service (IFS) and was India's Ambassador in Israel, Qatar, and France. After retirement, he served as India's High Commissioner to the UK until December 2015.

 Michael Arthur was a British career diplomat until 2010, when he retired as Ambassador to Germany, following his four-year stint in India as High Commissioner. Since then, he has held a variety of posts in the private and not-for-profit sector, based in London but travelling extensively.

 Asoke Mukerji was India's Permanent Representative to the United Nations, where he is credited with implementing Prime Minister Modi's initiative to have the UN declare an International Yoga Day within seventy-five days, with 177 co-sponsoring countries. The diplomat and author is a member of the International Institute for Strategic Studies (IISS) in London and a member of the Governing Council of the United Service Institution of India.

Ashok Malik is Distinguished Fellow at the Observer Research Foundation, New Delhi, one of India's leading public policy think tanks, and head of the Foundation's Neighbourhood Regional Studies Initiative. His work focuses on Indian domestic politics and foreign/trade policy, and their increasing interplay, both in the region and beyond.

Ashok has a background in media and is a prominent columnist for a variety of publications, including *The Times of India, Hindustan Times, The Economic Times, The Pioneer* and ndtv.com. In 2012, Ashok authored *India: The Spirit of Enterprise*, a study of the growth of the Indian private sector in the post-liberalisation period.

Lord Marland is Chairman of the Commonwealth Enterprise and Investment Council (CWEIC) and the Enterprise and Investment Company Ltd. He retired as the British Prime Minister's Trade Envoy and Chairman of the Business Ambassador Network in January 2014. He was Minister for the Department of Energy and Climate Change from 2010-2012 and subsequently for the Department for Business, Innovation and Skills.

Lt Gen Syed Ata Hasnain is best known for the stellar leadership he provided to India's Kashmir Corps in 2010-12, converting a negative situation to one of hope and peace through what he called the balance of hard and soft power. An experienced 'scholar warrior' in the field of modern day 'hybrid warfare', he is now a respected strategic analyst and public speaker.

Rahul Roy-Chaudhury is the Senior Fellow for South Asia at the International Institute for Strategic Studies (IISS) in London. He served in the National Security Council Secretariat in the Prime Minister's Office in the previous BJP government in India. He was on the faculty of the Institute for Defence Studies and Analyses (IDSA) in New Delhi.

Gareth Price is a Senior Research Fellow at Chatham House, leading research on a range of economic and political issues affecting South Asia since 2004. He previously worked as an analyst at the Economist Intelligence Unit, focusing on South Asia, and before that was the South Asia analyst at Control Risks Group.

Baroness Prashar is an independent member of the House of Lords, UK. Since 2012 she has been the Deputy Chair of the British Council. Her career has spanned public, not-for-profit and private sectors and she has made significant contribution to public policy and public life in the UK. She is passionate about promoting intercultural relations, diversity and equality. She has deep interest in the arts, culture and international relations.

Chandrakant Babubhai Patel is the founder of Asian Business Publications Limited (ABPL), the UK-based media house behind *Asian Voice* and *Gujarat Samachar* newsweeklies and the Asian Achievers Awards. He is considered a torchbearer for the British Indian community and has been involved with several organisations in various capacities such as Patron, Chairman, President and Committee Member. He has spearheaded several campaigns over the years, including to save the Hare Krishna Temple at Watford, London, and to lobby for the launch of direct flights from London to Gujarat. CB was awarded a gold medal by the Mahatma Gandhi Foundation for his long-standing community service and manifold achievements.

Sadiq Khan was elected Mayor of London in May 2016, winning the largest personal mandate in the history of British politics and securing the support of 1.3 million Londoners. Prior to this, Sadiq had a distinguished parliamentary career as the Member of Parliament for Tooting and also served as a government minister. Before entering politics and public service, Sadiq studied law at university and went on to work as a respected human rights lawyer for more than ten years.

Lord Desai is a well-known economist and author. He joined the Department of Economics at the London School of Economics (LSE) in September 1965. Since 2003, he is Professor Emeritus at LSE.

He was awarded the Pravasi Bharatiya Puraskar in January 2004 and the Padma Bhushan in 2008. He received the Jewel of India award from the Indian Merchants Chamber and is an Honorary Fellow of the LSE and a Fellow of the Royal Society of Arts. He has written over 25 books and divides his time between London, Delhi and Goa.

Lord Gadhia has over twenty-five years' experience investment banking experience, having held senior positions at Blackstone, Barclays Capital, ABN AMRO and Baring Brothers. He has advised on a wide range of high profile mergers and acquisitions, and capital-raising across developed and emerging markets, including some of the largest investment flows between the UK and India. He is a Member of the UK–India CEO Forum and the UK Advisory Board for FICCI.

Barry Gardiner is the Shadow Secretary of State for International Trade. His twenty years in Parliament have seen him hold ministerial office in three government departments: Northern Ireland, Trade and Industry and Environment. In 1999, Barry established Labour Friends of India and is its current Chair. Barry has led many trade delegations to India over the years and is a long-standing friend of Prime Minister Modi.

Barry did his first degree at St Andrews University before doing research at Cambridge University and Harvard as a John F Kennedy Scholar.

Barry also holds the distinction of being the youngest Mayor of Cambridge in the City's 800 year history.

Lord Bilimoria is an independent cross-bench peer and entrepreneur. In 1989, he founded Cobra Beer, which is now exported to forty countries worldwide and sold in 98.6 per cent of UK curry restaurants as a joint venture with Molson Coors. He is involved in many aspects of public affairs and higher education, as well as acting as Chairman of Cobra. Lord Bilimoria is a vocal campaigner for increased British overseas trade and was the founding-chair of the UK–India Business Council, Chancellor of the University of Birmingham, President of the UK Council for International Student Affairs and Chair of the Cambridge Judge Business School's Advisory Board.

Chandrajit Banerjee is the Director-General of the Confederation of Indian Industry (CII), India's leading industry association. He is a Member of the World Economic Forum's Global Agenda Council on India and also sits on the Board of the Commonwealth Enterprise and Investment Council (CWEIC). Banerjee is the recipient of the China–India Friendship Award and the Knight Commander of the Order of Queen Isabella by His Majesty, the King of Spain.

Patricia Hewitt is the Chair of the UK–India Business Council (UKIBC). As Labour MP for Leicester West from 1997 to 2010 and Secretary of State for Trade and Industry from 2001 to 2005, she made India her top international priority. She works closely with Katha, an NGO working with children in Delhi's slums.

Nikhil Rathi was appointed CEO of London Stock Exchange plc in September 2015 and also has Group-wide responsibilities for International Development. Rathi joined LSEG in May 2014 from the UK Treasury, where he held a number of senior positions over eleven years, including most recently as Director of the Financial Services Group, representing the UK government's financial services interests in the EU and internationally.

Anuj Chande is a corporate finance partner and Head of South Asia Group at Grant Thornton UK LLP. Additionally, he is the Global Relationship Partner for Indian key accounts. Anuj has over thirty-five years' professional and commercial experience. He has been recognised as one of Britain's 100 most influential Asians and has won the Lloyds Professional Excellence Asian Jewel Award.

Rajiv Memani is Chairman and Regional Managing Partner for the India region of EY. Rajiv is also a member of EY's Global Executive Board and Chairman of EY's Global Emerging Markets Committee.

Rajiv is active with many clients, principally with fast-growing Indian entrepreneurial organisations and global organisations establishing and expanding their presence in India. Rajiv is also a member of the National Council of the Confederation of Indian Industry (CII).

Jyotsna Suri is the Chair and Managing Director of Bharat Hotels Limited, which runs the Lalit Suri Hospitality Group. The Group is India's largest privately owned hotel chain. The Group recently forayed into the international market with The Lalit London. As past President of FICCI, Dr Suri is a multifaceted personality who believes in "developing destinations and not just hotels".

Nawal K Prinja has thirty-five years of academic and industrial experience in the civil and defence nuclear sector. He is the Technology Director of Clean Energy, AMEC Foster Wheeler, and is Honorary Professor at the University of Aberdeen and Brunel University in the UK. He chairs the Industrial Advisory Committee of the National Structural Integrity Research Centre (NSIRC) at Cambridge and has published three technical books and over forty-five technical publications. He was appointed as an adviser to the UK government to help formulate their long-term R&D strategy for the nuclear industry. Recently, he was invited by the Government of India as an expert to formulate their policy on science, technology and innovation for sustainable industrial growth.

Richard Gubbins is Senior Corporate Partner at Ashurst LLP and has been advising clients in India for over twenty years. Richard is a Director of AIM-listed Mortice, with two substantial businesses in India—Tenon and Peregrine—and is a Senior Adviser and Director of an Indian Family corporate office.

Gopika Pant is the Managing Partner of Indian Law Partners, dual-qualified to practice law in India and New York, with more than thirty-one years' experience working on cross-border transactions and matters. She sits on various Boards including GKN Driveline (India) Ltd, Xchanging Solutions India, and Asset Reconstruction Company (India) Ltd.